His Strong Hand

A BOOK OF ENCOURAGEMENT

Wendy Virgo

MONARCH
BOOKS

Oxford, UK & Grand Rapids, Michigan, USA

Published by Monarch Books
an imprint of
Lion Hudson plc
Wilkinson House, Jordan Hill Road,
Oxford OX2 8DR, England
Email: monarch@lionhudson.com
www.lionhudson.com/monarch

ISBN 978 0 85721 333 4
e-ISBN 978 0 85721 350 1

First edition 2013

Acknowledgments
Unless otherwise stated, Scripture quotations are from the Holy Bible,
New International Version Anglicised. Copyright © 1979, 1984, 2011
Biblica, formerly International Bible Society. Used by permission of
Hodder & Stoughton Ltd, an Hachette UK company. All rights reserved.
"NIV" is a registered trademark of Biblica. UK trademark number
1448790. Scripture marked NASB taken from the New American
Standard Bible®, Copyright © 1960, 1962, 1963, 1968, 1971, 1972, 1973,
1975, 1977, 1995 by The Lockman Foundation. Used by permission.
Extracts page 32 taken from The Grace of God by Judy Pruett. Copyright
© 1990 Judy Pruett/Kingsway Music tym@kingsway.co.uk. Europe
& Commonwealth (excl. Canada). Used by permission. And from
Salvation by Simon Brading. Copyright © 2007 Thankyou Music/
Adm. by worshiptogether.com. Songs excl. UK & Europe, adm. by
Kingswaysongs, a division of David C Cook. tym@kingsway.co.uk Used
by Permission

A catalogue record for this book is available from the British Library

Printed and bound in China, March 2013, LH06

To my three sisters

Contents

A Strong Hand

The views were glorious in every direction as we began to climb the Lion's Head. We had set out early while it was still cool and the conditions were perfect: a cloudless sky and, unusually for Cape Town, no wind.

The Lion's Head is a steep, prominent rocky outcrop next to Table Mountain, and can be seen from all round the city. From its northern side, it slopes away to form the back of a crouching lion. A conical hill topped by precipitous cliffs forms the head. At first the walk is relatively undemanding, spiralling around the rock and affording magnificent views over the city on one side, of the Atlantic on another, and down the Cape peninsula at the back. In the early morning light, the bays stretching southwards, the rolling blue ocean and the city lying under majestic Table Mountain were breathtaking. Cape Town is surely one of the most beautiful cities in the world.

As the sun rose, the heat grew, and the higher we got, the steeper the path became. By the time we reached a plateau just below the summit, I was feeling all my sixty-plus years! The last part looked extremely daunting. The grey rock was precipitous, and from where we were, it seemed practically vertical. The path we had followed was extremely narrow, and now getting to the top meant scrambling on hands and knees. I decided to give my shaking limbs a rest. To be honest, I thought I could probably reach the top, but was not sure I had the energy to face coming down. "You go ahead," I told the others. "I'll rest here and wait for you." So they carried on, climbing up the steep rocks.

After a while, I noticed that others coming up took a different route to the top. Instead of going straight up, they went round a bend to the right. I decided to investigate. It looked much easier, and eagerly I followed the path. But soon the trail petered out and I found I was in a precarious position. I couldn't go forward, but I couldn't face going down either!

Three people appeared behind me, panting. "There are some chains down there which you can hang onto if you want to go down," they said. Gingerly I inched down and saw where they had pointed. No way was I going to go that way – not on my own! It looked terrifying. I perched on a rock, trying not to look down too much, because that made me feel even more shaky. Suddenly I felt very alone. There was no sound, and the precipitous rocks seemed menacing in their silent grandeur.

I prayed, "Please, Lord, send someone to help me."

A tanned young figure appeared, climbing with the ease and vigour of youth. Swiftly he advanced from rock to rock. He saw me and grinned. "Can I help you?" he asked. "Are you going up or down?"

I explained my predicament. "I would like to get back on the path to the plateau, but I can't find it."

He reached out a strong brown hand and grabbed mine. "This way!" he said cheerfully. An amazing thing happened. The minute I put my hand in his, I felt completely different! I felt confident and secure. He hauled me up some steep places and shoved me round some boulders, and all my fear left me. That strong grip communicated assurance. Soon I was back on the familiar trail.

"OK now?" he enquired.

I nodded happily. "Yes, I'm fine." I was no longer lost or afraid.

Thinking about it later, I pondered on what made me feel so secure with him. He seemed utterly at ease on the mountain. He probably knew it well. He was full of energy and confidence, and he had a light-hearted, cheerful demeanour. He was enjoying himself. This wasn't an ordeal to him – it was fun! But most of all it was his strength which fortified me. It simply flowed through that large, comforting hand into my tired arms and legs, and I knew I would be all right.

The parable is obvious. We have a Pioneer who walks with us. We have been strolling along happily, but sometimes the path is very demanding and we can begin to feel a bit panicky. If we don't stick with our mountain guide we can get lost, frightened, stuck. Put your hand in the comforting hand of the man from Galilee.

Lotions and Potions

We are in Dallas. Terry is in a meeting, so I take myself off to a mall. After a pleasant hour or so of mooching around the sales in JC Penney and exploring various stores selling goods that I neither want nor need nor have any room for in my luggage, I am ready to take the shuttle back to the hotel. I congratulate myself that I have (so far) got away without spending any money. But first, I must find a large cup of coffee.

Astonishingly, it appears that there is not a Starbucks, or indeed, any coffee house in the place! I am wandering disconsolately down a hallway when a friendly young Jewish man leaps in front of me waving a tube of cream. Laughing, I attempt to push past him. I'm not going to fall for that old trick!

But he is determined, and I think, "What's the harm? I have time to kill anyway." So I listen as he rolls out the spiel. Special salt from the Dead Sea for exfoliation; miraculous cream that glides on and does wondrous things… and so on. I tell him I'm not interested, but he says, "Wouldn't you like to try just a little bit?"

Before I know it, I am sitting on a high stool, in full view of passers-by, as he holds my withered paw and briskly rubs a salty concoction all over it. He then wipes it off and applies the luxurious cream. He then invites me to smell it and feel my skin. It does indeed smell divine, and my skin is amazingly soft!

By this time, we are on first-name terms. I have told him why I am here in Dallas. He tells me he was born in Jerusalem. "Oh, wow!" I exclaim. "I was there last year!" Of course, this opens up a whole seam of conversation. What do I think of Israel? Where did I visit?

Naturally, he has also begun applying another miracle lotion on my forearm. It is a skin peel, meant for the face, but he kindly tells me that he wouldn't like to massage my face in public. I am so grateful, I let him continue.

By now we are talking about Jesus, a bit, in between inhaling the gorgeous fragrance of the potions and lotions. Eventually, I attempt to rise from the seat and extricate myself with my wallet intact. Naïve thought! As if…

He tells me how much the various pots usually cost. I gasp in horror, protesting that we have only just got rid of a mortgage, and I don't want another. Then he tells me the good news. "But for *you*, because I like you and you have been to Jerusalem, it will only be…"

No. No and *no*. Be firm, walk away.

Cunningly he then says, "But you do like it, don't you?"

"Oh yes," I say.

"Which one you like best?"

I shrug.

"You like this and this?"

I nod.

"I tell you what, special for you, I give you both for the price of one."

I falter. He goes in for the kill. Weakly, I nod. I produce my dollars. Oh, no... I will need change, I don't have the right amount... Too late! He sees the note, and casually suggests that if I buy a third product – for a huge reduction, of course – it will come to the exact amount of money in my hand!

Maths was never my strong point. I am now so confused, I am not sure what the bargain really is... if it exists at all! But I hand over the cash and he packs up my purchases nicely with tissue paper in a classy bag. Then he hugs me and kisses me on both cheeks. Evidently, we are now virtually family! We say goodbye with lots of affection and fervour. I have another stab at giving my testimony, to which he listens patiently.

"Well," I tell myself as I walk away, "I did pray before I came out this morning, and I did ask the Lord for an opportunity to witness. Maybe some seed was sown?"

Maybe a miracle will happen on my skin too! I

must say, the stuff smells wonderful and feels great. But I wonder if Yosef is now smiling about the elderly Christian lady who was ready to hand over an obscene amount of cash, as long as he let her talk… May her wrinkles ever increase!

The Cabin

I saw a clearing in a forest of tall conifers. It was dark in there among the trees, but sunlight poured into the clearing, where I could see a woodcutter in a red plaid shirt and blue jeans. He was swinging an axe and a pile of logs was growing nearby. As I watched I saw him split one right down the middle. Splinters of wood flew out and the wood inside was revealed, white and vulnerable.

He worked systematically, rhythmically, felling tree trunks, trimming off branches, cutting and splitting logs. Sometimes he took a smaller, more precise tool and worked more intricately, shaping and carving, and I saw what looked like banister knobs and chair legs beginning to emerge.

Then I looked behind the woodsman and saw a log cabin in the process of being constructed. Trimmed logs were fitted together to form the walls, floorboards were planed and smooth, and some furniture was already waiting to go inside. A beautiful house was taking shape – attractive in appearance, but also sturdy and strong to protect its inhabitants from the elements. It would be warm in winter, snug and cosy when the snows came down, an ideal refuge from storms.

Then I understood. It was a picture of the church. Jesus comes into dark places where barely any light filters through. He selects "trees" and cuts them down. Once tall and proud, rooted in their place, they are now his, to be used how and where he wants. Some may even be shipped out.

He takes individual tree trunks and cuts them into lengths. He has the plan of the church in mind and he knows where each log will be deployed. So he works – chopping, stripping, planing, carving. Some will be incorporated into walls, some into floors, some will be beams in the roof. Others will be worked on in more minute detail to be made into chairs and tables and cabinets.

All have their place, all are necessary. Elders and pastors are walls and doors; prophets are windows; some people are floors and get walked on all the time, but they are there to serve.

When the cabin is finished, it is finally ready to take on its primary function. Light fills it, smoke curls up from the chimney, smells of cooking waft out. It is not just for looking at; it is for living in. It is a home.

Over the door is a nameplate: "Emmanuel".

The Open Door

I was exhausted. We had moved along the coast from the small town of Seaford to start a new church in the much bigger town of Brighton. We had left our comfortable home and bought a huge, old-fashioned and very inconvenient Victorian house which had three floors and seven bedrooms. The high-ceilinged rooms were a nightmare to heat, and the kitchen was, to say the least, basic. The only other affordable housing was too small for a family with four children; this one had plenty of space!

We plunged into the complexities of church planting. Because the church did not yet have a building of its own, one of our bedrooms became the church office, and consequently there was a continual stream of people coming through our front door and up the stairs. With the many bedrooms there was always room for guests, and they came in droves.

Our youngest child was only three months old when we moved in. The two oldest had to be taken to school each day and met each afternoon. Usually I walked with them, pushing the baby in a pram, with Joel, the three year old, perched on top. There were always mountains of laundry and ironing to do, as well as the shopping and cooking for a family of six, plus a student lodger. The cleaning took forever, though I shall always be grateful for my friend Poppy who responded to my SOS for help. On top of all this, I was trying to get to know people, run a ladies' meeting, and breast-feed the baby.

I seemed to be constantly running: running to the shops, running up and down the long stairs, running out to the yard to hang washing on the line, running, running… Life was hectic and I began to feel exhausted.

With fatigue comes despondency, and a lack of perspective. You lose sight of goals, and live in survival mode, just getting on with the next thing on the list, forgetting why you are doing it, trudging along from task to task without a sense of purpose.

I reached a point where I hadn't read the Bible or prayed for days. Now guilt was added to the mix. I was the pastor's wife and I wasn't having a regular quiet time! I felt bad. I knew I should pray, but when?

Resentment now crept in. It wasn't fair! Praying just seemed like another burden to add to the heavy load I was already carrying.

Then one day I had a window of opportunity. The baby was asleep, and I had an hour before collecting the children from school. I could pray. Wearily I climbed the stairs to my bedroom, composing a nice prayer on the way: "Father, I'm sorry I haven't had time with you recently. I've been so occupied with these children you've given me, and all the church visitors and meetings…"

Reaching the bedroom, I shut the door and knelt by the bed. I was just about to embark upon my self-righteous prayer, when I began to see, in a vision, a massive oak door. It was slightly open. Cautiously I approached and timidly looked in. In front of me was a long room, and at the other end was a platform on which stood a great carved chair.

I knew Someone was seated on the chair. My heart sank. He seemed so far away, and I would have to trudge along what seemed like acres of floor to reach him. I could not lift my eyes to his face.

Then something wonderful happened. The figure at the far end of the room saw my nervous face peeping round the door and before I could take one timid step towards him, he leapt off the chair and came running down the room, with his arms outstretched. "Where have you been?" he shouted joyously. "I've missed you!"

I was totally melted. I forgot my careful prayer and spent the next hour laughing, crying and worshipping. It was one of the most precious hours in my life. Sometime during that hour he lovingly chided me, "Why do you shut me up here in your bedroom? Let me come with you when you walk to the school, or when you go shopping. I can be with you when you tend to the baby in the night, when you are cleaning and ironing."

This completely changed the way I had fellowship with Jesus. I found that the King of Kings is meek and lowly. He took a towel and washed his disciples' feet, and after that he often washed mine. He isn't too proud to help clean the bathroom, or sweep the floor.

Life is even more hectic today for many young women, as they have to go out to work in addition to running a busy household. Cultivating a relationship with Jesus can seem like another burden. We need to realize that the Christian life is not a formula; it is not "seven steps to success" or "six rules for victory". It is simply being with Jesus.

The disciples knew this. Mark 3:13–14 tells us that Jesus called to himself those whom he wanted, and appointed them "that they might be with him". Later, Peter could say, "Lord, we have left all to be with you" (Matthew 19:27). Being with Jesus was what it was all about. We tend to reduce the Christian life to hard work, routines, and belief systems.

We must know what we believe; we need convictions, and clarity about theology. But if we are not having fellowship with Jesus, it is all dry and meaningless. Jesus does not want to add to our burdens, he wants to take them away. This used to puzzle me. I did not understand that Jesus does not want us to just do things *because we have to*; he wants us to do things *with him*. We still have to work hard, but he works with us, sharing the load. You can talk to him on the way to the shops, in the middle of the night when you are comforting a teething toddler, when you are sweeping the kitchen.

"Come to me, all you who are weary and burdened, and I will give you rest... For my yoke is easy and my burden is light" (Matthew 11:28, 30). He shoulders the yoke, walking alongside us, a caring companion.

A Strong Tower

*E*arly in our married life we had many problems and difficulties as we slowly built our first church. Terry had received God's commission to build a New Testament church, but we had a very hazy idea of what that looked like. We and our friends had to learn together how to listen to the Holy Spirit, how to make room for one another's gifting, and how to love and respect one another.

We were also learning about the implications of biblical leadership and authority.

Church life was a process of bumbling along from crisis to crisis as some rushed ahead, others were cautious, and some were downright resistant to change!

It was a crucible of faith. Terry and I prayed constantly, both together and individually. Many times I saw Terry come in after a stormy elders' meeting, looking crushed and disconsolate. We had to learn to become more robust, and not easily offended or shaken. We also had much to understand about how the enemy hates, opposes, and seeks to destroy the church. A new church is a very delicate little plant, vulnerable to the vicious strategies which the enemy employs to crush it.

One day as I was praying, I had a clear picture of a tall brick tower. It was a simple cylindrical structure, with one doorway at the bottom, and slits for windows. As I prayed, seeking God's wisdom for whatever current predicament we were in, I saw myself run into the tower through the door at the bottom. All around the tower, the air was thick with arrows, spears, stones, and other missiles. There was the clash and clang of battle as they hurtled around, but inside the tower was safety and peace. Every so often a spear or arrow would hit the wall of the tower and bounce off. Sometimes one would stick in the wall or penetrate a slit: it could perhaps scratch me, or prick my skin, but its full force was spent on the wall of the tower. The tower was taking all the knocks and pain.

Proverbs 18:10 says: "The name of the Lord is a fortified tower. The righteous run to it and are safe." When threatened by any of life's hardships, we have a place to run into. How amazing that the Lord interposes himself between us and the enemy. He bears the full brunt of the assault. We are in Christ. He is our shield and our defence.

This picture became part of my defence against the barbs of the enemy. As I prayed, I would imagine myself running into the tower and pouring out my heart to God. As the Psalmist said, "Trust in him at all times, you people; pour out your hearts to him, for God is our refuge" (Psalm 62:8).

A Daughter's Decision

*A*nna had a day off school, I can't remember why. Anyway, it was December and I was making mince pies. Anna came into the kitchen and sat on the counter, swinging her legs and chatting as I weighed out the flour and looked for the rolling pin. At fourteen, with long curly blonde hair and blue eyes, and an expressive face with up-tilted nose, she was very pretty, and with her vivacity and zany sense of humour, it wasn't surprising that she was popular at school. She appeared to laugh her way through life and seemed more interested in planning and carrying out practical jokes than taking anything seriously.

She chattered away happily and I listened with half an ear as I measured ingredients. Then she said something which makes every mother's warning lights start flashing. "There's this boy at school, Mum. He's gorgeous, and he's asked me for a date."

"Oh?" I said, outwardly calm. "Tell me more! Is he in your class?"

"Oh no," she said airily. "He's in the sixth form!"

This meant that he was in the last year of school, and seventeen or eighteen years old.

"He's tall and funny," she went on, "and all my mates think he's gorgeous!"

I was beginning to get the picture. This godlike creature was obviously the object of adoration for most of Anna's friends, and to be asked out by him was a fantasy come true. To be asked out by a boy several years older was quite a feather in her cap, but to be asked out by this particular boy was prestige indeed!

"Wow!" I said. "And where does he want you to go?"

She mentioned the cinema. "I really want to go, Mum," she said.

Inside me, all sorts of agitated feelings were churning. I knew that it was important to choose my words with care. Now was not the time to screech, "You are not going anywhere near this guy!" Equally, I was also not about to congratulate her and push her out of the door. My instinct as a Christian mother was to protect and guide her, but I knew that she must learn to make her own decisions. My part was to steer her in the wisest direction. Whatever I said would be risky!

Praying for guidance, I encouraged her to talk. I began to slip in a few questions. What film would they see? Was she comfortable with that? Then gently I began to suggest some possible scenarios. "If he holds your hand, what will you do?"

She looked down and blushed, then shot me a

mischievous grin. "Hold it back, I should think!"

"If he asks you for a second date, what then?" I persisted. She was unwilling at first to think ahead, but eventually we began to talk about how she would feel if he wanted to put his hands in places that would make her feel uneasy. "Would you let him? Or stop him?" Bearing in mind that he was several years older, she began to realize that even if she felt uneasy, she would probably be too embarrassed to stop him.

"But Mum," she protested, "he's a nice boy! He wouldn't try anything like that!"

It was time to talk about our Christian convictions.

I explained that as he was not raised in a Christian home, there was no reason to suppose that he had the same sort of scruples that we might have. Our lives were shaped by our Christian values. His family, however good and kind they might be, would not have based their principles on the same values; therefore, if they had set boundaries, they would not necessarily be so clear or so important.

Anna's normally bright face became serious as she was forced to think through the implications of dating a non-Christian boy. She had been at school long enough to know what was normally expected of two teens dating. The question was, could she handle any eventuality and maintain her integrity? If they became really close, how close did she want to get? Could she cope with possible heartache? We also began to discuss what it means to follow God and do his will. It means believing that he has stored up things for us, and it is better to wait for his timing than to grab them before we are ready.

She began to see that every decision has consequences, for good or bad. She was also starting to see that it was her responsibility to make the decision, not mine. Making decisions is part of growing up.

Later in the afternoon, we climbed up to Chanctonbury Ring, an ancient clump of beech trees set high up on the bare slopes of the South Downs. We laughed and talked about Christmas, and cut twigs and ivy to decorate the house and had fun together.

Before she went to bed, Anna came into my bedroom. "Mum," she said, "I've decided not to go out with him. If I want to follow Jesus, I must do things his way. I think I'll say no to this boy, because it could lead to difficulties that I'm not sure I can handle."

I hugged her, my heart so full of thankfulness. The next day, she went and spoke to the boy, telling him frankly why she had decided not to go out with him – that she was a Christian and wanted to put God first. He was not a little surprised and somewhat embarrassed. Anna's friends thought she was mad. However, it was not long before some of her girlfriends began to confide to her some of their fears, guilt, and regrets over decisions they had made which had led them on to paths they had not wanted to go down. She had opportunities to pray with some of them.

And now? Twenty years later, Anna lives in beautiful Cape Town, married to a fine South African preacher, and is the mother of two sons and a daughter. She remembers that day as pivotal in her life, although at the time it was just a day in the life of a teenager. Maybe her life now would be very different if she had made a different decision then. Who knows?

Grace is Amazing

Terry ended his prayer, and the musicians came on stage. The audience erupted into joyful worship as Jordan led us into "The grace of God upon my life is not dependent upon me, on what I have done or deserved…"[1] We then moved on to sing Simon Brading's fabulous song, "Here I stand, with nothing in my hands, the best that I can offer, is a filthy rag…"[2] The declarations of gospel truth were accompanied by tears of joy, hand clapping, and unrestrained shouts as around 300 people worshipped Jesus for his amazing gift of grace. Terry had just concluded the last of three nights devoted to preaching his way through Romans chapters 5, 6 and 7, explaining the foundation of Christianity: freedom from the power of sin through the death and resurrection of Jesus, and the consequence that we are liberated from the demands of the Law to walk in the Spirit.

Yes: this is the very cornerstone of Christianity,

1. Taken from The Grace of God by Judy Pruett. Copyright © 1990 Judy Pruett/Kingsway Music.
2. Taken from Salvation by Simon Brading. Copyright © 2007 Thankyou Music.

and yet it is amazing that huge numbers of people who consider themselves to be born again are hazy about their freedom, and live lives regimented by laws which they impose upon themselves, or which zealous but misguided pastors impose on them. Many of us were raised in Godly homes, but our "Godliness" was measured by what we did on Sundays, where we went, or what we wore. In my early days, my sisters and I were not allowed to read secular books, knit or sew or listen to certain types of music on Sunday. Wearing lipstick (or any cosmetics) was considered to be "worldly" and was therefore not to be indulged in; and going to the cinema was definitely abandoning oneself to the devil.

At Bible college, I was sure I was saved; yet I believed that if I sinned I had to work through some self-imposed punishment to be acceptable to God. To confess sin and receive forgiveness just didn't seem adequate! Being filled with the Holy Spirit helped release me into a new and growing awareness of the grace and love of God. Terry and I often went to Westminster Chapel and were hugely blessed by Dr Martyn Lloyd-Jones' preaching.

But it was in the early days in the little town of Seaford, as Terry began to preach through Romans, that we came into an explosive understanding of the amazing truth that when Jesus died, we died in him. Our old lives were crucified at the cross, and when he was raised, we were raised with him into newness of life. He had borne our punishment and we no longer have to beat ourselves up to make ourselves better. We are not justified by works of law; we are accepted because of what Jesus has done for us, bearing our sins in his body on the cross. The Law, exemplified in Romans 7 as our overbearing husband, will never pass away; but we have died in Christ and the Law no longer has any claim on us. We are free to "marry" a new husband: Jesus!

There was an evening, probably in the early seventies, when the truth suddenly overwhelmed the small congregation. We leapt to our feet and sang and danced and praised God with utter abandonment. I don't remember how long this went on – it might have been hours – but I remember the heady joy and the shining faces of those who suddenly got a fresh revelation of Grace.

Since then, Terry has preached this around the world. Often people come to him in tears. "Is it really true?" they whisper. It's as if loads of invisible chains are left lying on the floor as they receive life-changing truth. It is not a new message; it is the message of the Gospels, of Paul, of the early Christian church, of the Reformers; it is the inspiration for thousands of men and women who have given their lives to announcing this truth. It is the foundation stone of our church planting, our discipling, our training, our evangelism, our marriages, our family life.

Sadly, over centuries, the gospel has become distorted and reduced to: "Ask Jesus into your heart, and then do your best to be good." What follows are various rules – which differ from place to place – that you are told you must keep to stay in God's favour. And they are all completely irrelevant!

After the meeting last week, people came up to me to say, "When I first heard this message, it changed my life." This happens every time. We were in Paris preaching it; in Dubai, in South Africa, Australia, India, Israel; in nation after nation the message of Grace has gone forth.

The Grace of God is liberating, powerful, never changing. It is truly amazing.

In Praise of Old(er) Women

"I shall be seventy on Friday!" whispered my friend during worship on Sunday morning. The last time I had seen her, eighteen months ago, she had been slowly recovering from a major illness, and had been pale and weak. Now, looking at her radiant, happy face, I thought I had never seen her look more beautiful.

As long as I have known her, Patty has always been attractive, vivacious, and a woman of faith. She has had many trials and difficulties but has prayed and praised her way through them.

Now, she rose from her seat, took the microphone and testified to the goodness and faithfulness of God, exhorting us to keep abiding in the Vine so we could continue to bear fruit. It was powerful, because she exemplifies her own words.

It took me back to Mrs Bendall. I met her when Anna, my daughter, had just been born. The elderly lady was a visitor in church that morning. She was quiet, a bit shy, but something about her made me want to get to know her. So during the week, I went to see her, wheeling the pram with Anna lying in it and two-year-old Ben perched on top. (Those were the days when we had prams built like coaches: high, with large wheels, and sprung so that the baby swayed gently, comfortably cocooned in the pram's inner depths – not stuck in a bucket on wheels, like they are now!)

I loved Mrs Bendall from that moment. She adored Anna, being very fond of babies, and often had her on her lap in church. Somehow, in her gentle, unassuming way, she became vital to our lives. She actually moved to live across the street so that she could be near us. She would pop in for coffee, babysit, and simply love us. Looking back, I can't think of any particularly wise and wonderful things she said; she just smoothed our way by lovingly serving.

She seemed to be able to communicate easily with anyone. She was very fond of cricket and always knew the latest test scores. I remember giving her a lift once, and also in the car was an inarticulate, awkward teenager. In no time this little old lady had charmed him into chatting away about cricket as if he had known her forever.

One day, she told me that she had not married until well into her forties. She was idyllically happy with her husband. Then just three months after their wedding, he dropped dead from a heart attack. I wept as she spoke with a gentle sadness, but no bitterness or anger. I remember the soft look on her face as she talked of the love of her life.

I wonder what fierce struggles she had fought and

won? Now there was simply a beautiful dependence on God, a deep trust, and a growing hunger for his presence.

One morning, we had an anxious phone call from her sister. Could we go and check on her? She wasn't answering the phone. We ran over and found Mrs Bendall's body lying on her bedroom floor – but she wasn't there. She had gone to Glory in the night.

We felt her loss keenly. I will always associate her with Psalm 92:12–14: "The righteous flourish like a palm tree… planted in the house of the Lord… They will still bear fruit in old age, they will stay fresh and green…"

Margaret Etherton was like that too. Always hospitable, she was a pastor's dream. She would stand near Terry at the end of Sunday morning and say, "Just send any people who need lunch down to me." We used to joke that her round table was elastic, as it seemed to stretch! She once made a chicken provide a meal for fifteen people. When we exclaimed, "How did you do it?" she just said vaguely, "It must have been the Lord…" It probably was. After all, if he could do it with loaves and fishes, why not a chicken? She was a woman of faith and prayer.

Recently, I had a letter from my aunty. She was 103 in August. She was widowed about sixty years ago, and had to bring up six children on her own. Now a great-great-grandmother, she is constantly praising

God and looking forward to meeting loved ones in heaven.

I haven't even mentioned my own mother, who at the age of eighty-two came to live near us. She had some cards printed inviting all the people in her block of flats to come to coffee. She gave her testimony to those who came and invited them to church. All her life she was motivated to bring people to Jesus, and prayed through every crisis.

I could go on, giving many examples of faith-filled elderly women. The thing is, now I am sixty-six, I am on the edge of being old myself! It is so strange, because I don't feel old. (I remember my grandmother referring to "those dear old ladies" who were in their seventies and eighties. She was ninety-eight at the time!)

People without God are terrified of old age because they know life is rushing to its end, and they don't know what to expect. So they try to perpetuate youth in an effort to postpone the inevitable.

Of course, there are unwelcome aspects to ageing: less energy, increased aches, droopy skin, wrinkles. I'm a sucker for face creams that promise miracles. (If you know of one that delivers the goods, let me know…) But the old ladies who walk with God have given me hope! You can be fruitful, happy, and serene, enjoying the advantages of growing old.

Yep, you have to be old(ish) to have grandkids, and

they are amazing! You don't have to prove anything any more, because you've been there and done that (whatever "that" is). And if you don't feel like rushing about, no one is surprised (although I still mostly do rush about). You have lots of good memories. You have lots to thank God for – and I do, all the time.

And you know what? We know where we are going. When this old body drops off, we shall be young again – or even better, recreated. I shall join the old ladies' tea party in the sky, except I won't be old any more. "Our youth will be renewed as the eagle's…" (Psalm 103:5).

Sisters

I am the eldest of four sisters. My father and mother had been married for just six weeks when he sailed with the Welch Regiment to India. He returned in 1945 and I was born in 1946, in Kingston upon Thames. Soon three others were born, and we spent most of our childhood in Maidstone, Kent.

Looking back, I can see now that post-war England was bleak and austere in comparison with today. But we didn't know that, and we were happy.

In those days, Maidstone was a small rural town, surrounded by hop fields and apple orchards and the North Downs. We had a long garden in which my father grew most of our vegetables. We kept chickens and ducks, which afforded us a lot of amusement as well as a steady supply of eggs. Behind the house, the ground sloped away over allotments down towards the River Medway. On the opposite side was a church with a tall spire, and often on a summer evening we could hear the sound of bells floating over the valley. However, we came from Brethren stock and walked the mile or so down the hill, over the bridge and round by the high walls of the prison to the plain little meeting

41

hall designed by my father. It's still there, but is now called an Evangelical Free Church. Being Christian was central to our family identity.

When we get together now, my sisters and I recall those far-off days with a mixture of nostalgic affection and amazement at our quite narrow and naïve upbringing; but also with huge thankfulness. Our parents were quite strict but we always knew we were loved. We had little in the way of material possessions; my clothes were hand-me-downs from my cousins, and by the time they reached my sisters they were fairly worn out! My mother was a gifted woman in lots of ways, but needlework was not one of her strengths, and I think she was often at her wit's end to know how to keep us adequately clothed. Consequently we had not the vaguest clue about dress sense. But as we lived in jeans most of the time, it didn't matter. We lived on roller-skates and bikes, mucked out the chicken house, and got roped in by Dad to help when he wanted to change the wheels on the car. I also helped him build a garage. Femininity? I don't think I encountered the word until I was about fourteen!

But we were always laughing. Yes, we did a fair bit of crying too, I suppose. A houseful of girls is never going to be a place devoid of emotion! We had huge arguments and fights, and competed noisily and energetically as we made up games, and slipped into being different characters for hours. We could be horrible to each other, but then if someone outside the family dared to criticize or hurt one of us, we would close ranks and vigorously defend each other.

When I left home to go to college in London, I missed my sisters like crazy. One by one we left, went on to further training, got married, and had children. We had had our rebellious moments, but we all married Christians and have all stayed with our husbands. Nearly all of us have reached our fortieth anniversary!

Now we are all grandmas. When I turned sixty, we got together for a weekend and enjoyed it so much that we have been doing it annually ever since. We love meeting and exchanging news about our families, books, and sometimes shoes, clothes, and jewellery. We shop, go for walks, eat too much, drink loads of tea and coffee, watch DVDs, and drink champagne! Last summer, we were at Sue's house in Ashford and we went to France on a day trip. It was raining, but when has that ever been a problem for four women in a shopping mall? I can highly recommend the Cité de l'Europe in Calais. Also the retail outlet in Ashford is awesome!

When the news broke in August 2011 about the riots and looting in some of England's major cities, I was so thankful for parents who loved God, loved each other, and loved their daughters. We were given boundaries and yet had freedom; we were poor yet rich by today's moral standards; we were smacked when we were naughty, but we knew we were loved. Now we are all parents, and grandparents, but our families have all been raised with similar values, and much prayer.

God invented family. He is "the Father, from whom every family in heaven and on earth derives its name" (Ephesians 3:14). I think it pleases him a lot when our families love each other and perpetuate that love from one generation to another. Strong Christian families are the glue which can hold society together, and the sad state of our nation has a lot to do with the fragmentation of family life.

Don't underestimate the power of a loving, God-fearing family.

The Covered Bridge

Years ago, Terry and I and some of our children were in Pennsylvania, USA, and it was there, as we were driving around one afternoon in the gentle rolling countryside, that I first saw a covered bridge. It looked a bit like a barn, with timber walls and roof, straddling a stream.

"Why a covered bridge?" you may ask. There are various answers. I was told that cattle crossing streams might have been frightened by the rushing waters, so the bridges were built to stop them seeing the water beneath. A more prosaic reason may be simply that the roof protected the wooden bridge from the weather, thus prolonging its life. Whatever the reason, the bridges are an interesting and often picturesque feature.

We were attending a conference at the time, and while we were worshipping, the image of the covered bridge kept intruding into my thoughts, until I began to realize that God was using it to speak to me.

What is a bridge for? It is a connecting point between two banks of ground, usually over a river. When you are on a bridge you are in transition: you

45

have left one side but have not yet arrived at the other. It is a vulnerable point. In war movies, bridges are often bombed because this disrupts progress and communication; supplies can't get through, people are marooned on one side or the other, and it generally hampers movement. In 2009 there were storms and floods in England, and in the town of Cockermouth, in the north-west, a bridge was washed away. This totally divided the community and necessitated a trip of several miles upstream to cross the river by another bridge. A journey which usually took ten minutes now took two hours! Bridges are strategically placed, but vulnerable.

In life, there are times when we embark on a new venture. We leave a familiar location in order to start something new. But a process is involved – one of actually leaving, walking across and arriving at the new phase. It might be the obvious change of leaving home as an adolescent and embarking on one's adult life. It might be making the transition from singleness to marriage by walking across the bridge of engagement. Pregnancy is like a bridge from being a couple to being parents. It may be about moving home from a town where we have been happy and comfortable to start again in a new place.

It is really about making decisions to leave the familiar, the known, the safe, and embarking upon the unknown, taking a risk, striking out into new territory. Some of these decisions can be made joyfully and enthusiastically; some are daunting and intimidating. Transition has an element of danger: on a bridge you are exposed to the elements, to bombs, to flooding waters.

As I pondered this, I heard the Lord whisper, "In me, all your bridges are covered."

It is he who asks us to strike out into new areas, to leave the comfort of the familiar, to stretch our wings, to be vulnerable. It is necessary for our growth and maturity. But "He will cover you with his feathers, and under his wings you will find refuge" (Psalm 91:4). In all our transitions, he is there, protecting us.

Through the Curtain

*I*went to see my Aunty Mary last week. She celebrated her 103rd birthday last August. She now lives in a home for the elderly called Pilgrims – which is appropriate for her, as although she is physically barely mobile now, she has a pilgrim's heart.

It so happened that I was near Leicester where she and several other relatives live, so first I called in on the youngest sister, Aunt Cicely, who is merely in her eighties. We were soon joined by her older brother, Uncle Jim, and then by two of Aunty Mary's six children, Diana and David, who are in their seventies. After a pleasant lunch in a local pub we all proceeded to Pilgrims and crowded into Aunty Mary's little room.

So what do half a dozen elderly folk talk about? There was a lot of laughter and gentle banter. David had recently driven home in fog, missed a bend in the road and somehow managed to go over a hedge into a field. The car was a write-off, but he calmly walked out and flagged down a passing car. My relatives are a tough lot! So there was some teasing about that. Aunty Mary, entirely lucid, asked after my own three sisters, remembering their names perfectly. Then there was some reminiscing about brothers and sisters, husbands and sons who have already passed on.

That was the cue for turning the conversation to the future. Yes, the past contains so many memories – some painful, mostly happy – but the future is wholly bright! What will it be like to slip away and wake up with Jesus? They were excited at the prospect! Now the talk turned to deathbed scenes – not macabre events full of fear and regret. Aunts Mary and Cicely were both present at my grandfather's death, some forty years ago, one on each side of the bed, holding his hand. He seemed to be unconscious, but they recalled how he suddenly opened his eyes and exclaimed, "Can you hear them? Can you hear them?" Then he said, "I'm coming!" – and a few minutes later, he breathed his last. What was it he could hear? What did he see?

Then last year, my cousin Richard, another ardent Christian, was dying of cancer. Shortly before he died, he asked, "Who is that man sitting over there dressed in white?" The others in the room could see no one; the chair was empty. Soon afterwards, Richard died. Diana remarked, "I think an angel came to escort him into Heaven."

Aunty Mary suddenly spoke up, her voice strong and confident. "It's so wonderful, and I still don't understand it. I am going to be with Jesus forever, but he is already in my heart! I have found that if you walk with him and obey him, he makes you happy." Profound truth simply expressed. When someone who has lived for 103 years says that, you listen!

I looked around the crowded little room on this bleak February day, at these ordinary ageing folk with their bright, happy faces. There was so much joy in the room! I was profoundly moved, and as I hugged them all goodbye tears filled my eyes. David prayed lovingly for me, for us all, and I left so grateful for such an experience, so thankful for being part of a Christian family, thankful for the wider family which is the people of God; and above all, amazed again at the wonderful victory of Jesus, who has broken the power of death, and given us hope for eternity.

Waiting

I don't like waiting. If I have to wait five minutes for a bus, I'd rather walk. My mother was the same. She was energetic up to the day of her death, preferring to walk rapidly, even run everywhere in spite of her eighty-four years. So perhaps it's in the genes.

But of course, waiting is part of life and cannot always be avoided. We have to wait for exam results, dental appointments, Christmas, a baby's birth; and mostly, these things cannot be hurried. Some we wait for with dread, others with eager anticipation.

We can wait anxiously for the results of a blood test; resignedly for the notice of a speeding ticket to arrive; impatiently in the queue at Tesco; eagerly for our wedding day; with longing for a holiday in the warm Mediterranean sun… or grumpily for a wet camping holiday to be over!

Psalm 130 is all about waiting eagerly, in hope: "I wait for the Lord, my whole being waits, and in his word I put my hope. I wait for the Lord more than watchmen wait for the morning" (verses 5–6). The word translated "wait" here is *qawal*, and the root of it is "to long for"; the sense is to wait for something you know will happen. David says he is putting his trust in God's word, which he will not go back on. So he can confidently wait for God's intervention.

There are several Hebrew and Greek words in biblical texts which are all translated by the same English word "wait". A slightly sinister word is *tsedah*, the root meaning of which is to do with hunting, and it is used when someone is lying in wait. Another word, *arab*, has a similar meaning, used to describe someone lurking, waiting in ambush.

The word *shamar* carries in it a sense of waiting watchfully, cautiously, to see what will happen. *Yachal* means to wait in hope, as does *shabar*. This is used in Psalm 104:27: "All creatures look to you to give them their food at the proper time" – a sense of creation waiting in dependence upon God to sustain and nurture it.

Then there is the word *duwmam*, whose root meaning is "to be dumb" – in other words, to wait silently, as in Lamentations 3:26: "it is good to wait quietly for the salvation of the Lord." Another very vivid word is *chakar*, which has in its roots the idea of adhering, sticking to, and is used in Habakkuk 2:3: "the revelation awaits an appointed time… Though it linger, wait for it; it will certainly come and will not delay." Isn't that graphic imagery? Don't give up on the promises of God: stick to them like glue. They will be fulfilled!

Why have I been looking up all these words? (By the way, it is worth getting a good concordance which lists words alphabetically, like a dictionary. Alongside each one is a number, and at the back of the book you will find the corresponding Hebrew or Greek word, its root meaning, and other usages.)

We are often tested and find ourselves unexpectedly waiting for something which is delayed. The way you wait affects the way you pray, and vice versa. "In the morning I will order my prayer to You and eagerly watch" (Psalm 5:3 NASB).

Terry and I thought we would have sold our house and moved to Kingston long ago. We put it on the market in February, and I thought, somewhat naïvely, that we would be settled by Easter. After all, God had spoken to us! He knew our busy schedule, the dates when it would be most convenient to pack up and go. He knew that we had the "Together on a Mission" conference to think about, and family coming and going…

He certainly did know; and I am grateful that he kept us in our house for the conference – it worked out just fine. But then, surely, everything would fall into place? Well, things began to happen, but there were frustrations and complications.

What can you do? Watch and pray.

We have to face the fact that we run into the same problems and delays and frustrations as anyone else in this uncertain world, with its economic perils and disasters. Sometimes we just have to wait. But there are different ways of waiting.

We can fume and seethe with annoyance; we can wait angrily; we can try to manoeuvre things; we can be negative and gloomy: "This is never going to happen, or if it does, it will be the worst possible time…"

We can lie awake at night worrying; we can be tense and uptight, living on the edge of panic: "Suppose we got it wrong! What's going to happen? How will we cope?" and so on.

For those with no hope in a merciful God who is a loving Father who plans the best for us, waiting is fraught with fear, anxiety and tension. But our Father tells us, "I know the plans I have for you… plans to prosper you and not to harm you, plans to give you hope and a future" (Jeremiah 29:11).

It honours him when we wait in faith and hope. He is the one who gives peace which is not dependent on everything going our way. He is the Prince of Peace!

So we can choose how we wait. I rather like David's way in Psalm 27:14: "Wait for [i.e. eagerly long for] the Lord; be strong and take heart and wait [i.e. confidently] for the Lord."

I also identify with Jehoshaphat when he was in a tight spot, surrounded by hostile forces. He prayed: "We do not know what to do, but our eyes are on you." The answer came back: "Stand firm and see the deliverance the Lord will give you" (2 Chronicles 20:12, 17). That's a good place to be!

Wedding Anniversary

*A*ugust 31st has significance for our family in several ways: it is the birthday of Hudson, one of our grandchildren; it is the birthday of my aunty, who was 103 this year; and it is my and Terry's wedding anniversary. We have clocked up forty-three years. Written down like that, it looks an enormous length of time, but it feels astonishing to me that so much time has elapsed, yet it seems to have passed so quickly.

Is it really forty-three years since I was putting on my lovely white dress, full of joyful anticipation? The phone rang. It was Terry, halfway up the M1, saying the radiator of his borrowed car had blown up and he was stuck at Newport Pagnell with his best man, the best man's wife, and their baby daughter. This was at about 12:30 p.m. The ceremony was at 2 p.m.

My already nervous father was dispatched in his car to race down the motorway, rescue them all, and try to get them to Leicester, all dressed and ready. Heroically, he did it. (Those were the years before speed cameras had been invented.)

So we duly had the ceremony, only slightly

delayed. After our seventeen-month engagement, I was simply euphoric that at last the day had come, and I floated happily down the short aisle of our Brethren assembly building to my waiting bridegroom, whom I hadn't seen for several weeks.

At the end of the wedding, we had a slight dilemma. The car was languishing somewhere near Newport Pagnell: how were we to get to Wales, where we had planned to have our honeymoon? This was where the resourceful Arnold Bell stepped in. He had been Terry's room-mate at Bible college, and had often jokingly enquired, "So, where are we going on your honeymoon, then?"

This turned out to be no idle speculation. Arnold now ran to the nearest phone box (no such thing as mobile phones in those days!) and called a farmer in the village where he was doing a locum pastorate. The farmer's cottage was free! So we, the newly weds, found ourselves leaving the wedding reception amid clouds of confetti in Arnold's car, and he drove us off towards Melton Mowbray. Terry and I had an idyllic weekend in a quaint cottage with roses round the door.

Eventually we made it to Wales as well, but we won't go into that! (Back in those days, many Christians did not feel free to stay in hotels, so we were in a Christian guest house… I think they have improved now. I hope so!)

You may think this was an inauspicious start, but

as it has so often been observed, a wedding is but a day, while a marriage is for life. I made vows on that day that I meant with all my heart, and there were times when I had to remind myself that this marriage was not just about me and my preferences: it was about solemn promises to one another before God. (This was in the days before marriage preparation classes had been invented.)

So yes, there were many adjustments to be made, as there always are when two sinful, selfish human beings attempt to live together. But when those two human beings are seeking to put God first in the relationship and are learning to respond to him as well as each other, there is grace to grow, grace to love, grace to forgive.

In a world where marriage is cynically regarded as just a bit of paper, where relationships end when the partners "fall out of love", where they don't know how to resolve differences, where there is sex but no friendship, where there is no respect, no laughter, no prayer… I am profoundly grateful that our marriage has been built on solid rock. I married a man who walks with God, and this makes me so secure.

My marriage is a rare and precious thing: it is not just a contract between a man and a woman; it is two people whom God has joined together to create a new thing, a unit that wasn't there before. It is a relationship which has the supremely high calling of depicting a mystery: the sacrificial love which Christ has for his church, and her wholehearted response of love to him.

Christians, guard your marriage well! It has the potential to say something to the world about God himself! People should see our marriages and be in awe. They should see two people who are still in love after many years, who love being together, never tire of each other's company, live in harmony although they are very different personalities, laugh a lot, pray a lot, are generous in attitude, give grace to each other and are protective of each other, and of this most precious relationship.

Surprisingly, after a disappointing summer, 31 August this year was a warm, sunny day. We had lunch at a pretty pub called the Golden Galleon, and then walked happily and contentedly hand in hand between the hedgerows down to the beach and back along by the Cuckmere River. The tide was high, and the water lapped gently on the banks. Larks sang in the sky and sheep dotted the smooth, rolling downs, basking in the hazy afternoon. It was blissful. So we strolled, my love and I, not talking of anything very profound, but deeply enjoying the moment, together, thankful for love and life.

I am so glad that God invented marriage!

Notes on Worship

The pastor of the church in Kenosha, an hour north of Chicago, called the chattering mob to order. "OK, folks! Time to stop talking and start worshipping!"

It was hard to get them to focus at first: 500-plus people all greeting, hugging, laughing, swapping stories, kids milling about. It was warm, friendly, lively, and strangers were welcomed gladly. But John the pastor persevered, and the band played some chords.

"OK, are you ready to worship? God is here. He will meet with us and speak to us."

Somehow you knew this was true; it had already been demonstrated in the expressions of love in the large auditorium. Now the people responded, rising to their feet to sing. For the next fifty minutes we were in glory, enjoying God, celebrating our salvation, worshipping the King among us.

A lot of the time our hands were in the air, or clapping, or both. The band was technically excellent: it was difficult to keep still! The words of the songs were declarations of truth that resonated in heart and mind. It was loud, but it seemed appropriate!

There were prophecies, a reading or two, a tongue and interpretation, a prophetic song. From the top of the banked seating to the front of the auditorium, there was enthusiastic involvement. Finally, it drew to a close. Fifty minutes didn't feel like a long time. When Terry came to preach, he was speaking to hearts that were open, primed to hear and receive.

At other times, I have been in worship that was technically excellent, but empty. I have been in long worship that seemed endless! I have been in loud worship, and it was simply noise that made my ears hurt. I have also been in worship that was efficient, brief and precisely timed. It did not leave me longing for more; there was no room for the gifts of the Spirit.

I have learned a technique: when I am in an unfamiliar crowd and I want to find Jesus, I imagine I am like the woman who needed to press through and touch his robe. I try to push through the obstacles to find him. But it is so refreshing when you are in a crowd that is shouting "Hosanna!" and metaphorically waving palm branches and welcoming the King! Seeker friendly? Bah, humbug!

So – how do you get there? You prioritize on the presence of God. Musicians learn that they are like priests who stand before God and the people, and make it easy or hard to find him. There has to be an ethos in the church of anticipating the presence of

God, recognizing him, cherishing him, and responding to him.

This church in Kenosha is a burgeoning church, a church on the move, but it's also a worshipping church. Gifts of the Spirit flow; lives are being changed; people are being saved.

I am so glad to be able to say that it is not the only one where such life is enjoyed. Churches are rising up around the world with these values. One of the promises that I love and pray about is that "the earth will be filled with the knowledge of the glory of the Lord as the waters cover the sea" (Habakkuk 2:14). Such churches edge us nearer to its fulfilment.

Babies

Babies. We love them, don't we?

I have made the long journey from London to Cape Town, mainly because of a baby; not just *any* baby, of course. No, this is my latest grandchild. You would have thought that maybe, already having a round dozen of them would dispose me to think, stifling a yawn, "So, one more to add to the collection. Now, what shall we have for lunch?" Not a bit of it! This one could have been the very first, I was so excited!

And lest you think it is just Grandma who is excited, let me tell you that when we got the message that Esme was finally in labour, Terry was prowling around muttering, praying in tongues, looking worried. We were staying in our friends' apartment in Lake of the Ozarks, Missouri, which was handy, because the eight-hour time lag meant that we were still in early evening, while Tim and Esme's friends in South Africa and the UK were tucked up in bed, as they should be at 3 a.m. the next day. So when the text message came that they were on their way to the hospital, we were the only ones awake to pray.

After a few hours, another message came that an

emergency caesarean section was necessary, so prayer continued with increased fervour. When the news finally flashed up on our phone screens that a baby boy was born and all was well, we hugged each other and cried with joy and relief.

Now here in Cape Town with little eight-week-old Boaz, we spend large amounts of time simply gazing at him, exclaiming at his beauty, loving the little coos and gurgles, and touching his velvety skin and soft, downy head. He is, without doubt, a gorgeous baby! But that's what we always think. Later, when they are grown up, we come across photos of them and with the objectivity that distance brings, exclaim, "Good grief, he looked like Winston Churchill!" But for now, we are besotted.

What is it about babies? They make noise; they make mess – often smelly mess. They can't hold a conversation, or play Scrabble, or football. They wake you in the night for drinks; in fact, they *demand* drinks without even saying "please". They burp, they erupt at both ends. All of these things would render them socially unacceptable if they continued to do them a few years later. In fact, we are at pains to educate them not to do them; but while they are babies, such behaviour is considered to be endearing and normal, and we willingly enslave ourselves to meet their every need.

So, why? Yes, I know, they are just so cute! But I

have isolated two things. One is the excitement and joy of new life, the links with what has gone before, and what is to come. The talk in the household is all about "I remember when you were a baby…" and "I wonder what he will be like?" Huge potential is wrapped up in this small person, at the moment so inarticulate, so immobile, so unable; and yet with a brain that has astonishing capacity to learn, a body that has amazing powers of development, and a personality yet to be discovered. It is like uncharted territory, virgin snow, paths yet untrod, unspoilt, unknown, waiting to be explored.

The other thing is the fun of seeing fleeting likenesses to the parents, who are one's own children. "Oh look! When he laughs/spits/frowns he looks just like Tim!" "He does remind me of…" There is something fascinating about seeing facets of ourselves reproduced in our children (it's a bit frightening too!), and even more so in our grandchildren. There is the intermingling of several family lines, and lo! a unique person emerges, yet with undeniable family traits.

God loves us, his children, like that. He knows what we have been and what we will be. We are part of a wonderful family that stretches back to Abraham and forward to eternity. He loves who we are now, but is working on us so that we become mature. He especially likes to see characteristics of his Son being displayed in our lives.

And another thing: we just love our babies because, because, because… God just loves us, because he loves us. He is love. I see Tim gazing at his son with such joy, yet he hasn't done anything to earn that love. Just his existence delights Tim.

The apostle John put it this way: "See what great love the Father has lavished on us, that we should be called children of God! And that is what we are!… what we will be has not yet been made known. But we know that when Christ appears, we shall be like him…" (1 John 3:1–2).

Be amazed at what we have come from; revel in God's love for us now; and live in the purifying hope of what is to come.

Daffodils and Other Smells

affodils! I love them. Bright patches of yellow that are like pools of sunshine, cheerful signs that spring is on the way! When I bury my nose in a bunch of them, I am transported back to the garden of my childhood home where they grew in the long grass under the apple trees.

Smells are so evocative. When I catch the fragrance of irises, I am standing in the corner of a classroom, a rebellious seven year old. I can't remember the misdemeanour that banished me there, but I well remember the impotent fury in my heart as I stood there for what seemed like hours, breathing in the potent aroma of chalk and wax crayons and the big vase of purple irises nearby.

Walking through airports, Terry and I always stop to have a squirt of expensive perfume in the duty free. We get on the plane smelling like millionaires, but can never remember which scent we really like, probably because we have tried too many and they are all mixed up.

Different places have distinctive smells too: the pine forest around the base of Table Mountain; the autumn woods near Arundel in Sussex; the grassy downlands reeking of sheep and thyme; the coconut sun lotion of sun-drenched beaches; and the strange and powerful mixture of aromas that assails you as you arrive at Mumbai Airport – dust, sewage, and curry!

It's amazing how the sense of smell enriches life. A certain furniture polish reminds me of my mother; cinnamon makes me think of America; and a whiff of a good red wine takes me to blissful days in the South of France or a vineyard in South Africa.

Of course, there are bad smells too: BO, bad breath, dog poo, dirty nappies, fields spread with silage... say no more!

Paul the apostle had the audacity to say that he was like a good smell. He said that when he and his friends arrived in town, it was like a subtle fragrance that made some people turn round and say, "Ah! What a lovely smell! It reminds me of Jesus!" On the other hand, others felt repelled and nauseated, because to them Paul smelt of death (see 2 Corinthians 2:14–16). How could he provoke such different reactions?

Often in the Old Testament we read of "a pleasing aroma to the Lord", and it is in the context of sacrifice. The smoke of the sacrificed animal wafted up to Heaven and pleased God. Why? A life laid down in worship, submitted to God, pleases him. Jesus taught that whoever loses his life shall find it, but whoever clings to his life shall ultimately lose it.

He modelled this; so that Paul could write, "Follow God's example, therefore, as dearly loved children and live a life of love, just as Christ loved us and gave himself up for us as a fragrant offering and sacrifice to God" (Ephesians 5:2).

It is true that to smell of Jesus is to smell of death: death to selfish desires, ambitions, and appetites. To choose to go through the narrow door is a kind of death, and not inviting to those who want to stay proud and independent. But to say "yes" to him, and in view of his mercy, to offer ourselves as a living sacrifice, holy and pleasing to him, is the way to life.

You want to smell good? Die! Choose Life!

God's Surprises

My youngest son has hit his thirtieth birthday. He was born at 6 a.m. on a snowy day in January 1982. After a hard night's labour, I lay in the hospital bed, looking at the little blue bundle in the cot beside me, glad that it was all over, and a bit bemused that we now had five children. This was not our idea!

Ten years earlier we had had a boy, then a girl – Ben and Anna. We also had a very small income and a small house, and two children were just about manageable. So for a while we felt that we probably had our quiverful, but were not entirely closed to having one more. Then one day a lovely family visited us who had three teenage boys and a little girl. They were such fun, and when they left, we looked at each other and said, "Let's go for four kids!" So we did; over the next few years Joel and Simon were added to the family.

We were complete! The last one was duly potty trained, and with a sigh of thankfulness I put away the nappy bucket (this was in the days before the ubiquitous Pampers). I could now emerge from babyhood and toddlerdom. My nights would no longer be dominated by feeds and teething wails; my body could shrink back to its normal size; I could sit down to eat instead of shovelling porridge into the baby and gulping food haphazardly while standing up; a small(ish) buggy would suffice instead of a big three-wheeler. Babies are great: cuddly, sweet, but hard work! I'd had enough!

I was packing up baby clothes to give away, when six-year-old Joel wandered in.

"What are you doing, Mum?"

"I'm packing up baby things to give away. We're not going to have any more babies."

He looked at me in horror.

"Not going to have any more babies? I'm going to pray about that!"

Joel doesn't remember that; he is now a pastor, preacher, and father – and a praying man. But even then his prayers were powerful. A few weeks later, I was completely astonished to find I was pregnant! In fact, I was devastated.

I went to the doctor, who confirmed I was pregnant.

"Was this baby planned?" he asked.

"No," I admitted.

"Well, you already have four. We could see if you have grounds for a termination," he offered.

I was shocked. In that moment, I knew that such a course was not only against all my doctrinal beliefs, but it violated something fundamental in the core of my being. Inside me was an embryonic human child, being grown, nurtured, protected, prepared for a life. How could I be party to destroying it? All my instincts were marshalled to protect it. This had nothing to do with convenience, with putting my life on hold, with plans for a tidy, symmetrical family.

I went home with a different perspective. Terry prayed and God spoke to him, saying this child would be a joy to us. We had a name picked out: Nathan. But when he was born, we looked at him and said, "This isn't a Nathan!" Somehow, we knew he was to be Timothy.

Now Timothy is a man. Just writing those words chokes me up! He has come to maturity. He has married a beautiful, Godly young woman called Esme, and they are serving God in Cape Town. Now they have a son called Boaz.

Boaz!? That was a bit of a shock, until Tim explained that Boaz in the Bible was noble, kind, gentle, uncompromising; a kinsman-redeemer, a picture of Jesus. OK. I think I can live with that!

I am glad God had another plan that superseded our plan. If we had had our way, Timothy would not have existed, and neither would Boaz. Not only is Tim a joy to us; he has a little family which expands the joy!

God often surprises us; his ways are not our ways. Abraham had to wait until he was a hundred before he got his son, in whom were wrapped promises for the world. Mary gave birth to her son, the promised Messiah, in a cowshed. The sons and daughters born to us all have enormous potential to further God's purposes on the Earth. God's word says that children are a gift from the Lord (Psalm 127:3). Keep that in mind when yours are driving you up the wall, and pray them into the destiny that God has planned for them.

Hampton Court

*O*ne Monday, Terry and I went to Hampton Court. This Tudor palace beside the River Thames, built by Cardinal Wolsey and later acquired by His Majesty Henry VIII, is absolutely vast. We walked around in it for four hours and only saw a fraction of it.

It was also cold. Outside, it was grey, cloudy, and cool: typical London weather. We thought we would be warm and sheltered inside. Sheltered from the brisk breeze, yes, but not warm! The Tudors did not enjoy the benefits of central heating, or any heating, apart from huge log fires in the main galleries. Alas, in frugal, recessionist, twenty-first-century England, such luxuries are definitely on the cutback list: the tourist must suffer for his or her culture by shivering.

The corridors are wide and draughty, the halls have ceilings like cathedrals, and many of the floors are stone. Not cosy. The Tudors began to stir my deepest sympathy.

I had to wonder: how did the king manage to seduce all those women in such arctic surroundings? Maybe they were all so desperate to get warm that if he invited them into his chamber where there was a fire, they trampled on their scruples and rushed in, holding out blue, chilblained hands to the blazing logs in the hearth!

However, the palace is extraordinary. It has its own quite large and imposing chapel, labyrinths of rooms, huge kitchens, quadrangles, squares, and fountains. We didn't have time to visit the famous maze, the original Tudor tennis court, or the extensive gardens and water features. They will keep for another time on a warm (please) day. But there is something awesome about walking in a place that is redolent of history, imagining the halls and corridors full of servants scurrying about, the imposing courtiers clad in their padded doublets and hose (so that's how they kept warm!), and the imperious cardinal swishing through the throngs in his flowing crimson robes. I could be walking where Anne Boleyn once danced!

In Tudor times, it took a papal legate months to get to Rome and back; no wonder the King's divorce took so long. What would have happened today, with jet planes and emails? Anne Boleyn on Facebook? Everything would have been immeasurably speeded up. Maybe as a consequence Anne's life would have been even shorter. Hmmm…

It was deeply fascinating. I felt proud of… well, perhaps not, but definitely awed, by our ancient heritage. To be part of such a long line of humanity is both humbling and inspiring. I enjoy learning about days gone by, and how our present place in the scheme of things has come about. But exciting as those days were, there was also cruelty, ignorance, prejudice and pain, as indeed there is in every era. Terrible things happened then, as indeed terrible things happen today. Every time has its own greatness, good and bad.

On the whole, I am thankful that I was born "for such a time as this". I am thankful to live in a time when one can have warm baths, and turn on the heating; where clothes are easily washable; where there is a variety of food and knowledge of good nutrition; where there is pain relief in childbirth; where everyone learns to read – in fact, where girls receive equal education to boys; and where we can read the Bible without fear of being beheaded.

Yes, the past is fascinating, but the present is where we are, with its challenges but also many benefits. Tudor England was colourful, dramatic, and full of inconsistencies; terrifying too. There are lots of reasons why I am glad to be alive right now!

Everlasting Lists!

I have been reading in Nehemiah. This morning, reading chapter 8, I somewhat groggily suspected that I had read this stuff quite recently. Granted, it was early and I was half asleep, but I riffled back a few pages and there, sure enough, in Ezra chapter 2, was an identical genealogical list of people who returned from exile to rebuild the temple. This isn't the most riveting bit of the Bible... so why is it included twice?

That got me thinking about other seemingly interminable lists of names in sections of Joshua, Judges, Samuel, Kings, and Chronicles, as well as Ezra and Nehemiah. These are not passages that are often preached about; in fact, I have rarely heard them alluded to at all! They are full of pitfalls for unwary preachers, containing many unpronounceable names, and not much that is other than yawn provoking.

But it got me wondering: why are these meticulously compiled lists included at all? Do they enhance our understanding of humankind – our rebellion, our lost plight? Do they reveal truth about atonement, justification, righteousness? Do they help us to live better lives? Well, maybe not overtly. But they do show us that the Bible is not a random set of myths, as some would suppose. It is about real people doing real things: mostly about begetting children, it's true, but also about building walls, taking land, creating cities.

These lists are so carefully compiled that there are often cross references to support their accuracy, and footnotes with alternative spellings. Every jot and tittle has been accounted for, and however tedious it may seem, there is hard evidence here for historical fact.

But it also excites me to know that I have ancestry: I belong to a tradition of those who lived by faith, who entered into the promised land, who fought for their inheritance, who just got on with having babies, and continued the chain of families in the people of God.

God knew every one of their names and wanted them recorded. They not only had existence, they had faces. Sometimes interesting little details are inserted in the lists – for example, Jabez (1 Chronicles 4:9–10). His name means "Pain" – not a desirable tag, one has to admit. Yet he is remembered for a remarkable prayer: "Oh, that you would bless me and enlarge my territory! Let your hand be with me, and keep me from harm so that I will be free from pain." His mother suffered; apparently he suffered too, but he cried out to God for big blessings in his life! What is more, God heard and granted his request.

Some were listed as skilled craftsmen; others were musicians; some were gatekeepers who guarded the threshold of the temple. Others were mighty hunters, or warriors. Some were prophets, some were priests. Whole tribes are listed, and clans and families within them.

I sometimes wonder about the scribes who had the job of keeping all these records. Who were they, and why did they? Presumably, they were appointed for the job. Did they actually count every person? And did they count the camels, goats, horses, sheep, and cattle? They too are often listed. Such detail!

I'm glad it wasn't my job. I am not a details sort of person. I do not delight in the minute debris of life: numbers, train timetables, knitting patterns, washing-machine manuals; forms for passports, bank accounts, insurance. I find them tedious and boring. Yet they are necessary and important, and irritating though they are, life would be infinitely more muddled and confusing without them.

The lists in the Bible show me something of a God who cares about individuals, who takes trouble over details. His lists are not impersonal, random inventories, but careful accounts of real people who created history. Our history. He made a path through the Red Sea; he sustained a nation for forty years in the desert; he shut the mouths of lions, sent fire from Heaven, inspired mighty warriors. But he also knew when Jabez prayed in his pain; he knew that Benaiah killed a lion in a pit on a snowy day; he knew all the people who are just obscure lists of names to us: Eliezer, Reuben, Shemaiah, Zabdi, Ezri, Azarel... who married who, and who their babies were.

He knows me too, and you. My name is written in his Book. In fact when Jesus, our Great High Priest who ever lives to intercede for us, holds up his hands, all Heaven can see your name and mine, and countless others, graven on his palms.

We are known, owned, and loved.

Nomads and Pilgrims

(Written on a long trip in the USA)

I feel a bit like a nomad these days! I am beginning to identify with the children of Israel as they moved from place to place. But the similarity ends there, because they encountered near starvation and acute dehydration from lack of drinking water. That doesn't happen so much in the USA. In fact, the danger is over-abundance of food and drink. More choice and availability than you can handle!

Also, I am very glad that we travel in comfortable cars rather than on foot, or donkey, or cart. Driving in the States is fun: cars have lovely adjustable seats which heat up in cold weather, holders for coffee cups, and space for coolers bursting with snacks. (Americans get nervous if they are not plentifully supplied with snacks.) The roads are often wide, straight highways, relatively uncrowded. A long ride (to us Brits) of six or seven hours is a pleasant opportunity for congenial conversation, with plenty of stops for more food and drink. And, especially if you are in the north-west, there are stunning views to be enjoyed.

Compare that with England: for example, the legendary M25 with its permanent, crawling rush hour, irritated drivers, cafes and loos few and far between, and the prospect of arriving totally exhausted after three hours of frustration. So being a nomad in the USA is not so bad!

But it's not just the going, it's the arriving: constantly packing, unpacking and repacking; wishing you had left at home half the stuff you are carrying, and regretting things you didn't bring; trying to juggle moving from temperatures of 80 degrees Fahrenheit to 25 and back to 75; sleeping in many different beds. Mostly, I've found that the beds are great – it's the pillows that cause problems: too many, too few, too soft, too hard… yep, I'm picky. Kay Valentine's in Missoula, Montana were the best so far – soft and squashy, but with enough substance to give neck support. I'm not moaning, I'm deeply grateful. The Israelites probably didn't have pillows at all! We have been looked after, fed (well!), loved and cared for. We are blessed.

Where am I going with this? As well as "nomad", the Bible uses another word: "pilgrim". Actually, a pilgrim is slightly different from a nomad. A nomad simply wanders. A pilgrim travels with purpose. He or she has a destination in view. A nomad's vision is as far as the next meal, the next B and B. A pilgrim sees each stop as a milestone on a journey. Psalm 84:5 says,

"Blessed are those whose strength is in you, whose hearts are set on pilgrimage." Pilgrimage requires vision, determination and faith. A pilgrim has seen something and is motivated to go after it. "By faith Abraham, when called... obeyed and went..." He was looking for a city. Similarly, "By faith Joseph... By faith Moses..." (Hebrews 11:8, 10, 22, 24).

Which are you – a nomad or a pilgrim? I think I want to be a pilgrim.

The Joy of the Whole Earth

Our first real damp, drizzly autumn day. We are in Idaho now, up in the North-west USA, with its wide, open spaces, conifer-clad mountains and placid lakes. There is a sharpness in the early morning air, the mountains are crowned with mist, and even in the thin rain the trees are glorious in their deep crimsons, golds and yellows. It is so different from the mania of LA, our last stopping point, with its nightmare traffic cruising at 60 m.p.h. on six-lane highways, snaking over and under in convoluted systems – except during rush hour (which is most of the day), when it crawls bumper to bumper and a short journey can take two hours!

We flew via Salt Lake City – a strange place, like a Lego town dumped in the desert. From the air, Utah is like a lunar landscape: brown sand broken with outcrops of red rock, and scarred with dry, wriggly water courses. The Lake itself, when I saw it, was smooth, undisturbed by waves. No boats made wrinkles on its surface, and it was strangely coloured: reddish, then pale blue, then beige, then mauve. An eerie, alien body of water.

But here, in Idaho, the water is reassuringly normal! And even on a wet day, the landscape is beautiful in its autumn glory.

The variety of this great country is never-endingly fascinating, and we are so privileged on this trip to see so much of it. We have yet to have a brief break at Yellowstone National Park, then on to Dallas, and eventually ending in Mexico. But my abiding impression is of a more enduring beauty. Wherever we have gone, the greatest joy has been to be with the people of God.

Psalm 48:12–13 says: "Walk about Zion, go round her, count her towers, consider well her ramparts, view her citadels…" We have visited several expressions of "Zion" in the last few weeks; in fact, we have seen many such expressions all over the world in the last few years. We have spent time in Grace Church, Sydney; in Jubilee, Cape Town; in Jubilee, St Louis; in Christ's Church, Ozarks; in God First, Johannesburg; in our churches in Wellington and Christchurch, New Zealand, in Dubai, in Paris, France, in Manila, in Guadalajara, Mexico; and, of course, in many churches in the UK.

Some we have spent months in, some only a few days. But it is a wonderful thing to land in an airport a long way from home, and to see a smiling face, to be greeted by brothers and sisters in Christ, to be welcomed into their homes, to share meals and stories of what God is doing, to laugh, cry and pray together. It is wonderful to be in a worship setting and feel, "This is where I belong, this is home."

Home? Where is home? Yes, we need a place of permanence, a context where we especially belong; but we also need to see that any earthly home is temporary. Don't cling too close... it could be destroyed at any time, or the Lord could ask us to move! There is only one home that will endure – the dwelling place of God; and while we are upon the earth, the church is the expression of that for us.

I have discovered that as Terry and I travel around so much, it is easy to get disconnected, to stand back and become a spectator. I can enter yet another church building and look around, thinking, "Hmm, the welcome wasn't so good here... Plastic chairs! They need to get some new ones!... The notices were way too long... I don't know any of the songs – I don't like them either... The band is too loud..."

But you don't get fed, you don't grow, you don't edify anyone with that sort of attitude! I want to be eagerly expectant: whatever "body of Christ" I am with today, I want to be there with faith.

"Great is the Lord, and most worthy of praise, in the city of our God" (Psalm 48:1). The church is Jesus' joy, his passion. More than all the beauty of this planet – the mountains, streams, seas, sunsets, and autumn leaves – he loves the church! I want to love the church too.

So I sometimes remind myself as I enter another church, "Glorious things are said of you, city of God!" (Psalm 87:3). I will position myself to hear God, to worship God, to be alert for prophecy, to be involved as a member of this body. Today this is my church, and all my springs of joy are in it (Psalm 87:7).

Beautiful Feet

Spring is here, so it's time to review the summer shoe collection!

I love summer shoes, but at the same time I am apprehensive about putting my ageing hooves on display. Each year my toes appear to be more bent and my bunions seem more prominent! I am always on a quest for shoes that are pretty and elegant, but not crippling to walk in. Consequently I have amassed quite a collection; I have shoes for different seasons, shoes for different climates, shoes to go with dresses and shoes to go with jeans and trousers.

I tip them out of the box: the black, the white, the heels, the flats, the wedges, the trainers. I sigh regretfully because I do not have beautiful feet!

In the Bible beautiful feet are not about shoes and footwear, but about what they do: they run! They carry the heralds of Good News! "How beautiful... are the feet of those who bring good news, who proclaim peace... who say to Zion, 'Your God reigns!'" (Isaiah 52:7).

In Luke's Gospel we read about a woman who was so bent over that her vision was confined to the ground. She couldn't see whole people, only feet. For eighteen years she had been imprisoned by a condition which caused her body to be bent and rigidly locked. One day she shuffled to the synagogue. As she made her way painfully to the back, behind the screen where the women sat, she heard a man's voice: "Woman!"

She knew in the depths of her being that he was calling her. Slowly, embarrassed yet compelled, she stumbled forward into the midst of the crowd.

"Woman, you are set free!" Something unlocked in her heart. Years of grief, disappointment, and rejection fell off her. Who was speaking? She could only see his sandal-clad feet – dusty, calloused from walking miles over rough terrain. To her they were beautiful: they belonged to the bearer of Good News!

Then she felt his hands on her gnarled and twisted back. A current of energy, like a wave of warm water, flowed over her, and the tight, fused vertebrae began to pop and loosen. Pain ebbed away, and she began to uncurl and straighten up. Amazed, she found herself standing tall, her stick on the floor. No longer was she looking at his feet; she looked into a face beaming at her with tenderness and delight.

Others standing around did not share her joy. Their backs were straight but their minds were crooked, and their perspective was cramped and limited. They were indignant because healing had taken place on the Sabbath!

Jesus spoke again: "Should not this woman, a daughter of Abraham, whom Satan has kept bound for eighteen long years, be set free...?" (Luke 13:16).

He not only healed her body; he gave her dignity and identity.

Today, Jesus still comes to make the crooked straight: crooked bodies, distorted thinking, skewed perspectives, twisted attitudes.

One day we too shall see those feet; they have been wounded, they have holes from nails driven through them. But to us who have received Good News, they are so beautiful. And we shall also look on his face, because he has made the crooked straight, and we can stand unashamed before him.

Yet, somehow, I think we shall also spend a lot of time prostrate at his feet.

Airports and Henry

I love airports: but sometimes I hate them. I hate them when I have arrived at an insanely congested airport in an unfamiliar city, where I have to stand in line for hours in Immigration, eventually to be processed by an unsmiling individual who makes me feel like an insect that has just walked into his country.

I hate it when I have to wait in a huge queue for my bags to go through the X-ray machine, and I have to take off my shoes, my coat, my belt, take out my laptop, even my make-up bag, walk through and be felt all over by an unknown woman, and then reverse the process. It is so degrading for everyone involved.

But this morning, as I drove into Heathrow Terminal 1 to meet my son-in-law, I felt a tingle of excitement. It may have been something to do with the fact that several things worked today. For example, I was actually early. The last time I met Steve, just before Christmas, I got stuck in traffic so horrendous that I was nearly despairing of life itself by the time I got there. In company with thousands of other motorists, I am sure I wasn't the only one wondering if I would have to camp out in the slow lane until Spring arrived and everything would get moving again.

Another thing was that today, for some reason, there was plenty of space in the car park. The terminal was quiet and I could get a cup of coffee and wait in comfort. Such minor things conspired to make my mood positive and bright. Plus, of course, I was meeting Steve!

So yes, a good vibe! There is something exciting about being in a context where people are converging from all parts of the globe on one spot. You watch the monitor and see a flight has just landed from Riyadh, another from Los Angeles. One is about to leave for Frankfurt, another for Mumbai. It all seems so exotic, and suddenly it is possible to be anywhere but here! Of course, the truth is that in those places there are also endless waits, frustrations, terrible traffic chaos, and infuriating bureaucracy.

But I think I get the tingle, the wanderlust, the itchy feet because an airport is like a gateway to other possibilities: hot climates (top of the list for Brits!), interesting cities with intriguing architecture, different cultures, different accents, different food, different vegetation, different everything. Every country has its own "feel" and flavour, each to be sampled and savoured; yep, even the UK, no doubt.

Some years ago, back in the nineties, Terry and I were visiting a dear friend in hospital. Henry Tyler was not just a friend, he was a legend. He had been a pastor for many years before he joined us in our newly developing church in Brighton. He became part of the leadership team and brought experience, love, wisdom, and prayerfulness with him. He also had a great preaching gift and theological depth and knowledge, from which we benefited enormously. He was also a Godly and loving pastor.

Now he was in hospital, painfully living out his final days on Earth with kidney failure.

I remember, he didn't look good: weak, thin, yellow. But he still smiled and joked; he was happy. He had written a book called *Jump for Joy* which always epitomized him, as he was a happy man. Now, lying there, near the end, he was not only happy, he was excited. He had refused dialysis. "What's the point?" he said. "It would prolong my pain for a few weeks! I don't need to hang around. I'm in the departure lounge. I want to take off!"

A few days later, he did. I believe he arrived in a country that is altogether different, but recognizably, welcomingly, home. For Henry, who loved to travel, but who also loved home comforts, it must be perfect!

I often think of him, when I am in a departure lounge.

Rugby for Grandmas

Sport is an obsession in Cape Town, and they start early in life. My grandsons, Joshua and Ben, have rugby practice after school a couple of times a week, and often have a match on Saturdays too.

One afternoon I found myself alone with Ben while his brother and sister were elsewhere. Ben is cunning; he is nine years old, has melting brown eyes and a cheeky grin, and is very beguiling. "Shall we go for a walk in the park, Grandma?" he said.

The walk in the park somehow evolved into him riding there on his bike while I trotted along carrying a rugby ball, and another cone shaped object which Ben seemed to think was important. Most of the park is occupied by multiple rugby fields, cricket pitches and tennis courts. We reached one of the rugby fields and Ben laid down his bike by the goalposts. "I'm going to practise goal kicks, Grandma," he announced. Now I understood the significance of the rubber thing I had been carrying. It was a cone which holds the egg-shaped ball in place, preparatory to a player kicking it over the bar between the posts.

Ben began practising his kicks while I ran about

retrieving the ball and sending it back to him. Not too demanding, and good exercise! But then Ben decided we would vary it a bit by doing drop kicks. This is one of the more dramatic aspects of the game, when the player with the ball attempts a kick at the goal while running. It has an element of spontaneity, and when it comes off in a game, it is very exciting! So we tried drop kicks for a while. Ben got more over than me, but I was quite good, considering.

However, Ben now decided we must progress to passing. The ball must be passed backwards, not forwards. So the player with the ball runs forward with it, and passes it to a player slightly behind him. So my relentless coach had me zig-zagging up the field, throwing the ball behind to Ben, then running around him and catching it as he threw it back to me. Then as we approached the goalposts, Ben attempted to drop kick the ball over the bar. We did this a few times, and when Ben got it over he leapt about triumphantly. I was lying down.

"Come on, Grandma, let's do it again!" he shouted to my figure, lying prone and heaving on the grass.

"Give me a minute!" I gasped.

A minute was all I got. My coach waited impatiently while I hauled myself into a sitting position. "You're just not fit, Grandma!" he said severely.

Meekly, I got up and we repeated the process a

few more times, but by the end, I was walking rather than running.

Fortunately, I never got initiated into the scrum; and when he mentioned that I might learn to tackle, I hastily declined. "I'm bigger than you," I explained kindly. "It wouldn't be fair." We staggered home – or rather, he rode his bike and I staggered.

On Saturday, Ben was playing in a real match. The opposition was strong and fast. At one point, one of their forwards came steaming down the wing with the ball. Ben, playing full back, streaked across and brought him down with a superb flying tackle. Oh joy! It was right by the line where I was standing, so I got a great view. Ben got up, but before he got back into the game, he turned and gave me a beaming smile of pure happiness.

One for you, Grandma!

The Lion's Head Revisited

Well, I did it. Cue drum roll and trumpet fanfare. Third time lucky, I made it to the top of the Lion's Head! That may not mean anything to a lot of people, but those who have visited Cape Town will appreciate my sense of triumph!

The Lion's Head is a spectacular peak on the west side of Table Mountain, 669 metres (2,200 feet) above sea level. It is roughly conical, and its top portion is composed of a precipitous wall of granite rising almost vertically.

There is a path which winds around and up to a shoulder, about two thirds of the way up. I have made it as far as that twice before, but have been defeated by the last demanding and terrifying stretch. The climb to the summit is a scramble on hands and knees, pulling oneself up by the fingertips, inserting toes into crevices. It also involves a couple of iron ladders thoughtfully placed on the steepest bits.

It was a Sunday afternoon. Terry and Steve were watching Manchester United playing Everton, and Anna and I decided to go for a walk. We thought a stroll along a beach would be pleasant, but as we drove over towards Camps Bay, we thought, "What about having another go at the Lion's Head? Maybe today's the day to crack it!"

Conditions were ideal: a clear, warm, sunny day with just enough of a gentle breeze to keep us cool. So we set off on the path which winds round and up the spectacular rock, and gets steeper and more demanding the higher you go. The views were breathtaking.

Eventually we reached the plateau on the shoulder below the summit, where I had got stuck twice before. By this time I was feeling all my (nearly) sixty-six years and was tempted to give up again. But I have a determined daughter. "Come on, Mum, you can't give up now!"

We started scrambling up the steep ridge. "Don't look down! Just look at the rock in front!" She didn't need to tell me twice. Pure, unalloyed fear gripped me. I found also that I didn't have the agility I once had and could not haul myself up. "It's no good," I lamented despairingly. "I just don't have the strength."

Just then, some people came up behind us, but went around to the right and moved on up. "Let's follow them!" we decided. To our surprise, we found a better way, a more defined route, which, although it involved hands and knees and some real climbing, was accessible.

Much encouraged, we ascended, and twenty minutes later, after much puffing and panting on my part, we emerged at the top! We could see a full 360 degrees: across Table Bay itself, with Robben Island (where Nelson Mandela was imprisoned) lying in the shimmering water; then further west out over the Atlantic, down southwards to Cape Point, where there is nothing but ocean between the tip of Africa and the South Pole; then sweeping round eastwards to the Indian Ocean and the mountains of Somerset West, until you face due north up the continent of Africa. It was a special moment, standing there contemplating that amazing scenery.

We phoned our couch-potato husbands and informed them of our location. Yup, they were surprised. The descent was quicker and easier, and we returned feeling sore and tired but triumphant.

Thinking about it afterwards, what did I learn? Why did I succeed this time?

Several things stood out. One was the power of encouragement. "Come on, Mum, you can do this!" Another was following others who knew what they were doing; their confidence reassured us.

I also found that Anna's instruction to keep focused on the next step and not look around (especially down!) was good advice. If you are distracted by other details, if looking down makes you dizzy, your strength seems to ebb away. I was also worried that I might make it to the top, but I wouldn't be able to get down.

The main thing was to achieve the goal: to get

to the top! We need goals, ambitions, and challenges which draw out of us strength which we didn't know we had. Paul the apostle said, "forgetting what is behind and straining towards what is ahead, I press on towards the goal to win the prize for which God has called me heavenwards in Christ Jesus" (Philippians 3:13–14).

As you get older, you inevitably slow down a bit, but you don't have to stop. It's good to ask ourselves from time to time, "Am I still pressing on? Do I still have ambition for the kingdom of God?" Not only that, but is there someone I can encourage whose strength is flagging, who is in danger of giving up, who is in danger of being diverted? We are in this together; let's encourage one another!

"Even youths grow tired and weary, and young men stumble and fall; but those who hope in the Lord will renew their strength. They will soar on wings like eagles; they will run and not grow weary, they will walk and not be faint" (Isaiah 40:30–31).

Breakfast on the Beach

B reakfast out of doors is unusual in England, for obvious reasons, so it feels somewhat exotic and special. One of the most enjoyable features of Cape Town is that there are lots of lovely places to eat breakfast. There are lovely little street cafes where you can really stuff yourself on what is ironically called "the full English" for the equivalent of about £4. Then there are stunning places like Groot Constantia, where you can sit under a tree by the ancient Dutch-style wine cellar, with the view spread out before you towards Muizenburg Bay, the mountains forming a spectacular backdrop.

Then there is the decadence of the terrace of the Radisson Hotel, right by the ocean, where you can watch dolphins while you munch your salmon and scrambled eggs. One of the best places for breakfast is at the Rhodes Memorial on the slopes of Table Mountain, where you gaze due north across Cape Town to the rest of the world.

You can see that there are reasons for going to Cape Town besides visiting the family!

Back in England, where the rain tips down

relentlessly, my mind went to a familiar Bible story (John 21). It was early morning by the Lake of Galilee. As the light was beginning to dawn, two boats were drifting into shore. The fishermen were exhausted. Cold, hungry and fed up, they had been fishing the whole night without catching anything. But they were also downhearted because they had lost their sense of direction.

As the sun came up, they saw a wisp of smoke spiralling up into the still air. Someone was evidently making a small fire on the beach, and as they watched, they saw him throw on some more twigs. He called across the stretch of water, "Hi! Have you caught anything?"

"No!" they shouted back despondently.

"Try throwing the nets the other side!" he called back.

They did, and caught a massive shoal of fish that threatened to swamp the boat! The man looked vaguely familiar, and John suddenly exclaimed, "It's the Lord!"

Immediately, Peter tugged on his coat (I have never understood why he did that), jumped overboard and swam ashore. As he splashed onto the beach, he began to smell the appetizing aroma of fish grilling, and new bread. Ahhh!

By now they had all recognized that it was Jesus who was tending the fire and cooking fish over it. He simply said, "Bring some of the fish over here and I'll cook some more."

Peter went over and helped his mates haul in the net, which was full to breaking-point. Then they all straggled over to the fire and sat around it, rubbing their cold hands.

Jesus handed round bread and fish, and gradually they warmed up and began to feel more relaxed. Breakfast on the beach! Suddenly the day which had started so drearily didn't seem so bad. Jesus was there!

They felt warm and well fed and happy. The long cold night had not been in vain; they had a good catch. They laughed and talked with their mouths full. But still, I think they were a little in awe as they received fish and bread from hands that had big holes in them.

It always surprises me that Jesus was so practical and down to earth. He had some pretty big issues to talk over with his confused disciples. They had all run away when he had been seized by the Roman platoon; Peter had denied, with cursing, that he had ever met Jesus.

As he sat now by the fire on the beach, I wonder if Peter's mind went to another fire in the courtyard of the fortress where Jesus had been dragged to be flogged; and if he squirmed as he remembered the curious stares of the serving girl who thought she recognized him, and the cold, naked fear that overwhelmed him;

and the piercing sound of a cock crowing in the dawn of that terrible day.

Yet here was Jesus, risen from the dead, with the scars visible on his resurrected body, calmly handing round barbecued fish!

He had been dead and was now alive; he was divine but still human. He knew that before he confronted them about major issues, they needed breakfast; they needed time to adjust, food in their bellies, warmth, ordinary conversation. This was the third time he had appeared to them, but it was still pretty unsettling! Food, especially fish, frequently seemed to be involved in reassuring them that he was really, solidly present, and not just a dream.

Jesus waited until they had finished eating, and then he turned to Peter and gently began to probe. "Do you love me, Peter?" They needed to talk, but by caring for Peter's physical needs, Jesus brought him to a state of mind where the thing that was bothering Peter most could be brought to the surface and dealt with.

Don't you love it that he cares about every detail of our lives, the small and the great? Often it is his attention to those small things that melts our hearts and opens us up to bigger things.

"Do you love me?"

"Yes, Lord, you know that I love you."

I think I would like to have breakfast on the beach with Jesus.

A Monument in Berlin

Wide, tree-lined streets; trams; high blocks of flats; expensive shops like Gucci, Ralph Lauren, and Versace; little street cafes and the obligatory McDonalds; gracious old buildings; vast paved squares and spacious parks... Berlin is a great city and I loved my brief experience of visiting it.

Terry and I were met at the airport and taken to an impressively large, modern train station, soon to disembark at another massive station with high, domed glass ceilings and endless escalators. We went out onto a huge, empty square and across a bridge over the river to a wide, grassy space in front of the Reichstag, an impressive building where the German government meets. Badly damaged by bombs in the war, the ornate front façade survives but is surmounted rather incongruously by a high glass dome; the juxtaposition of the old and new seemed rather uncomfortable to me.

We walked on and soon came to the famous Brandenburg Gate, standing in a commanding position at the meeting point of several wide avenues. It has become symbolic of the triumph of democracy since the fall of the infamous Berlin Wall in 1989, when it was the scene of euphoric celebration as the Wall was torn down. We wandered around with other tourists, taking the obligatory photos on both sides of the magnificent monument. But before we took the tram back to the hotel, there was one more monument to see.

Just a block away from the Brandenburg Gate lies a strange and sombre sight: a great square filled with grey rectangular blocks of stone, identical in length and breadth, but not in height. They are symmetrically laid out on a sloping site, somewhat reminiscent of a graveyard, but no words or numbers are carved on them. They lie under the sky, mute and anonymous, some high, some low; and although the pathways between are straight and regular in length, the floor is undulating.

There are 2,711 of these blocks, and people wander around among them, gravely, thoughtfully, sadly. There is silence apart from the background sounds of city traffic. The whole area is a monument to the millions of Jews who were shipped by train from all over Europe and murdered in the concentration camps.

The site is an in-your-face confrontation, a shocking, unavoidable reminder of a crime so horrific that it seems unreal. We wandered about among the slabs, reassuring ourselves that it was a long time ago: it wouldn't, couldn't happen now. Then it dawns on you:

it was only sixty-five years ago, just two generations – not that long ago! In fact, it was uncomfortably recent.

So, could it happen again? The sad truth is that something like it is happening somewhere in the world all the time; perhaps not on such a horrendous scale, but in a way that is just as cold-bloodedly calculating and callous. For example, we have seen the "ethnic cleansing" in Serbia and Bosnia; the civil war between Hutus and Tutsis in Burundi; the systematic slaughter of innocents in Sierra Leone; the killing fields of Cambodia and Congo... the list goes on. And these have all been in the last twenty years or so. Do human beings never learn? It appears not. They do not educate themselves out of murderous hatred, fear and prejudice.

In a serious mood, we climbed on board the tram and made our way to the flat rented by the courageous Nigel and Claire Dutton and family, who have gone there to plant a church. Here we mixed with forty or so people from all walks of life and several ethnic backgrounds. Together, we worshipped Jesus, listened to his word and prayed to him who is the only One who can change hearts and fill them with love and compassion.

Many peoples will come and say, "Come, let us go up to the mountain of the Lord... He will teach us his ways, so that we

*may walk in his paths." ... He will
judge between the nations and will settle
disputes for many peoples... Nation will
not take up sword against nation, nor will
they train for war any more.*

Isaiah 2:3–4

Here is Hope. Let your kingdom come, Lord!

Another Look at
Hudson Taylor

*O*ver the years I have read several biographies of Hudson Taylor. The first one I read when I was about eight years old. Coming from a missionary-minded family, many of the books and stories I was exposed to from an early age were about Christian pioneers. So I read about David Livingstone, Amy Carmichael, and William Carey. I read avidly and widely; but those missionary books gave me a taste for biography and history, and I still maintain that fiction rarely improves upon real life for adventure, courage and surprise.

I have just finished reading a new biography of Hudson Taylor. He was born in 1832, before the age of steam, motor cars, telephones or even efficient sanitation. His father was a chemist, and also a preacher of the gospel in the villages surrounding Barnsley in Yorkshire, where the family lived. Hudson was mainly educated at home by his mother but eventually worked with his father in the chemist shop. He became a committed Christian at the age of fifteen, and began to nurture a desire to go to China to bring the gospel to the Chinese.

From then on, everything he did was focused on how he could best prepare himself for this task. He lived as simply as he could, eating frugally, saving money, and seeking to toughen himself physically. He decided to study to be a medical doctor, because that would help to open doors and make contact with people. He also learned to trust God for the necessities of life. Eventually he sailed for China on 19 September 1853, on a ship from Liverpool.

The ship was very nearly wrecked before it left the Irish Sea, encountering violent storms, and emerged only to go through another ordeal in the Bay of Biscay. The whole voyage took nearly six months!

When Hudson arrived he met with other missionaries who had been working in Shanghai, but his desire was to move further inland into uncharted territory. He encountered fear and suspicion from the Chinese people, who had never seen an Englishman, and who called foreigners "white devils". He found it was easier to be accepted if he wore traditional Chinese clothes, and so he got rid of his English frock coat and trousers and took to wearing wide, baggy pants and a long tunic. He shaved the hair from the front of his head and grew the back hair long enough to plait into a pigtail (or queue). He worked hard at becoming proficient in speaking Chinese; and of course, this meant adapting to the numerous dialects in different towns.

The Western settlements generally despised his efforts to become like the people he was seeking to reach, and it caused a good deal of controversy. But as time went on, it became obvious that his methods were fruitful, and they became the accepted practice with the missionaries who followed him.

Over the years, thousands did follow him. His wholehearted devotion to God and to the Chinese inspired men and women literally to lay down their lives in China. It is heartbreaking to read of those who endured the long voyage, knowing they were unlikely to see their families again; and then died within a few years or months of malaria, cholera, or in childbirth. Hudson Taylor himself lost several children, and his beloved first wife, Maria, died after they had been married twelve years.

Hudson himself suffered physical pain from injuring his back in a fall on a boat, and frequent bouts of dysentery which left him weak. He endured misunderstanding, and being the subject of vicious rumours. Stories circulated among the Chinese that the white Christians stole babies and ate them. Harder to bear were libellous reports from fellow missionaries accusing him of bad motives, and even immorality.

He returned to England after about seven years and, burdened about the massive task of evangelizing the nation of China, was walking and praying one day on Brighton beach. The outcome of that day was that the China Inland Mission was formed, and the next day, a bank account was opened in that name with £10!

What he achieved almost defies belief. He travelled incessantly as an itinerant preacher, and later he visited mission stations which had been established all over the vast nation. Everything he did came out of prayer and was bathed in prayer. Famously, the mission he established, the CIM, never asked publicly for funds; they only asked the Heavenly Father, and proved him to be a generous and faithful God.

Later, in the early twentieth century, there was great conflict and unrest in China and many missionaries were killed. Yet the work continued and churches not only stood firm but grew.

Although I had read the facts before, while reading this new book I was struck afresh by several things. One was the sheer hard work of this man and of those who worked with him. They never stopped sharing the gospel, praying, and teaching, while living and travelling under appalling conditions. Coupled with that, they were entirely selfless, always thinking of others, never indulging themselves, giving of their possessions, their time, their energies, their very lives! They were utterly devoted to Jesus: his love was what compelled them.

It has become fashionable to criticize what we now call "old style" missionaries. Certainly, I am grateful for renewed understanding of the church, and the establishment of church communities, which does away with some of the dilemmas raised by "para church" missionary organizations. But I am in no doubt that these nineteenth-century missionaries were truly led by God, sustained by God, and glorified God with their sacrificial lives.

Things are so different now. Our high view of marriage and family life would not lead us nowadays to separate ourselves from husbands or wives or children for long periods of time in order to make lengthy journeys to inhospitable places to share the gospel. Also, some of their views and methods would seem distastefully "colonial" in the present day. The globe has "shrunk" in the sense that however far away we may travel, we can go virtually anywhere on the planet and be only days away from home. We can communicate by phone, email, and Skype; and even in the remotest places we can be in touch and receive help for medical emergencies far more quickly than they could.

Yes, the contexts have changed; the veneer of civilization, culture, and human progress has made life easier in many respects. I wouldn't want to go back to the nineteenth century! Yet I deeply admire those "old style" missionaries, and can't help asking myself if I, in my generation, am as passionate and focused as they were?

What courage! What self-denial! What obedience! What faith! What devotion to Jesus! Surely these will earn his "Well done, good and faithful servant!" They were like the heroes in the book of Hebrews:

> *They went about... destitute, persecuted and ill-treated – the world was not worthy of them... Therefore, since we are surrounded by such a great cloud of witnesses, let us throw off everything that hinders and the sin that so easily entangles. And let us run with perseverance the race marked out for us, fixing our eyes on Jesus...*

Hebrews 11:37–38; 12:1–2

We have to run our race, in our day, in our culture. But Jesus is worthy of no less devotion.

Numbering Our Days

There is something fragile, bittersweet, about nostalgia, a wistful longing to recapture what has vanished. We enjoyed the moment, and we want to preserve it. It has enriched our lives, we savour the memory. We had a great day on the river… a wonderful steak dinner with friends… the baby grandchild took his first steps. We want to freeze-frame it, stretch it out, slow the clock. Stop, please stay, let me extract one more drop of pleasure from you!

But it's gone! Passed by. We can't stop the earth from turning in its inexorable cycle. The funny thing is that as you get older, time seems to go quicker. As a child, in June, Christmas seemed aeons away. Now I'm in my sixties, we seem to have only just put away the decorations, and already Christmas is looming again! The years hurtle by, and suddenly you have a son of forty, grandkids at secondary school. You wake up, look in the mirror, and see your mother staring back. It's shocking!

This is a recurring theme in the Bible. Moses, Job, David, Isaiah, James, Peter: they all comment on the fleeting nature of life. "The life of mortals is like grass, they flourish like a flower of the field; the wind blows over it and it is gone, and its place remembers it no more" (Psalm 103:15–16). Mortality; brevity. Did I even make a smudge on the page of history? As Isaac Watts' hymn says:

> *Time, like an ever rolling stream,*
> *Bears all its sons away;*
> *They fly, forgotten, as a dream*
> *Dies at the break of day.*

Another log floats by on the flowing stream of time!

So I am intrigued when I read that with the Lord, time is different. He uses another system for measuring. "A thousand years in your sight are like a day that has just gone by, or like a watch in the night" (Psalm 90:4). What does this mean? Truly, the Lord is not tied to an earthly timescale, and literally, there is a different concept of time in eternity.

But I also wonder if it could mean that God sees days whose significance stretches into infinity, because a man or woman believed him and obeyed him even in a small thing, and that action continues to grow and bear fruit. Some days which we think are unimportant, he invests with great significance, so that their usefulness stretches way into the future, while others we thought significant have already been lost in oblivion.

We are faced continually with having to make decisions. Life rolls on, and years later we look back and realize that a relatively small decision affected not only our immediate personal history, but had a cumulative impact that is still active in the lives of many others. I do hope that in eternity we get to see a rerun, and if so, that we will begin to appreciate events from God's perspective. We shall see what he counts as truly of lasting worth. I think we shall be in for some surprises.

Psalm 90 is a prayer of Moses. In it he prayed, "Teach us to number our days, that we may gain a heart of wisdom" (verse 12). As he looked back, what did he see? His days as a prince in Egypt; the day of the burning bush and God calling him to deliver Israel; the parting of the Red Sea; striking a rock and streams of water appearing… What momentous events! But they were set in motion on a day when his mother plaited some reeds and wove a basket, and with a breaking heart put her baby in it and launched it on the river.

There was a day when a young apprentice shoemaker told his friend William Carey about how he had become a Christian, and invited him to church. There was a day when a mother was praying for her son, Hudson Taylor, and God apprehended him; a day when Martin Luther, a young monk tortured by guilt, read, "The just shall live by faith", and was saved by grace through faith.

There was a day when Terry was sixteen, when his sister told him she had become a Christian, and led him to put his trust in Jesus.

We number our days: by birthdays, anniversaries, graduations. We look back at them, how? Sick with nostalgic longing for days long gone? With regret for opportunities not taken? With bitterness for injuries sustained and never dealt with? Through rose-tinted glasses which make the past always seem so much happier, more carefree? With pride for some achievement?

In it all, how faithful God has been!

Let's learn from our memories; be thankful for the blessings, learn from mistakes, forgive the hurts, and grow wiser. Then we can face the present, saying, "This is the day the Lord has made. I will rejoice and be glad in it."

Live in today! Savour the love and mercy and goodness of our God!

A River Runs Through it

Oklahoma City is situated in the hot, dry plains in the centre of the United States. The heat can be extreme. Last summer the temperature was over 100 degrees Fahrenheit for sixty straight days. But in the winter the harsh winds sweeping across the plains can make it bitterly cold.

Previously, my only perception of Oklahoma City had been through the famous Rodgers and Hammerstein musical, *Oklahoma* – "corn as high as an elephant's eye", "wind rushing down the plain", women in bonnets and gingham dresses making up baskets, covered wagons, and farmers and cowboys fighting each other. Yeah, well, it might have been like that 150 years ago!

Now it's still windy and lots of corn is grown, but the discovery of oil has brought in money. Today, Oklahoma is a big modern city: banks, hotels, parks, and a beautiful new skyscraper soaring up over fifty floors and dominating the landscape.

But it's still dry and hot! What do you need? Water! Fifteen years ago, a lone and apparently deranged terrorist bombed part of the downtown inner city. The city council decided to redevelop the devastated area and more besides, and consequently, pleasant parks and plazas have been made, and especially a pretty canal area lined with walkways, trees and flowers, restaurants and bars. It's a good place to stroll, hang out, have a drink, or tour on one of the pleasure boats.

Flying over Oklahoma State to Colorado, the terrain is flat and treeless. Red earth begins to give way to dusty brown. Occasionally a dark-green scribble meanders over the monotonous plains, evidence of a stream where grass and bushes mark the watercourse.

Water transforms a city. So many cities are built, for obvious reasons, on riverbanks: London, Paris, Basle, Chicago, Warsaw, Rome, Budapest, to name a few. We have moved from Brighton, on the coast, to live in London. I miss the ocean but I am happy to be near the River Thames.

Psalm 46 speaks of another city which has a river running through it. "There is a river whose streams make glad the city of God" (verse 4). John the apostle also saw it in his vision: "Then the angel showed me the river of the water of life, as clear as crystal, flowing from the throne of God and of the Lamb down the middle of the great street of the city" (Revelation 22:1–2).

The city of God is built around the river of God. Our churches should be communities through which the same river runs – the presence of God which sustains, fortifies, refreshes – the source of life. It should be possible to identify where the water is, because that is where there is evidence of life. In the physical, trees and grass mark it out; in the spiritual context, the water of life can be seen by the fruits of the Spirit in the lives of believers.

We need constantly to replenish our souls' energy. The water of life pours out from the throne. So let us draw near and position ourselves under the waterfall; let us bathe in the river, drink deeply of the living water! We have the promise that "Water will gush forth in the wilderness and streams in the desert" (Isaiah 35:6).

From a Distance

The heat was sweltering. We sat in our air-conditioned condo in Missouri, USA, and – oh, joy! – found, after flicking through countless channels, that ABC TV was reporting on the Queen's Diamond Jubilee in London, England.

Naturally, rain was pouring down! Naturally again, the crowds lining the riverbanks and holding street parties were stoically cheerful under their umbrellas. I almost felt guilty for being in the heat of a Missouri summer; almost.

It was odd to be watching it from America. The gold-and-crimson barge carrying Her Majesty moved slowly down the River Thames, followed by a flotilla of a thousand smaller boats. Heroically, and incongruously, a rain-sodden choir persisted in singing "Land of Hope and Glory" from one of the boats as the flotilla arrived at the Tower of London. The brave, diminutive figure of Her Majesty stepped ashore, scorning an umbrella. I guess her wide-brimmed hat provided some protection.

We watched more of the celebrations two days later when the Queen and her family went to St

Paul's Cathedral for a service of thanksgiving for her reign of sixty years, followed by her procession back through the packed streets, and her appearance on the balcony of Buckingham Palace. Excitement mounted as the vast crowd, estimated at 2 million, poured down the famous Mall and jostled for a good view of the balcony.

I was riveted, excited, moved, because by rights I should have been there. I am a British subject! My father fought in World War II, and I was raised to revere the Queen and the institution of the monarchy. But I was watching from a long distance, thousands of miles away in another country.

I have an affection for America. I love my friends there, I enjoy (mostly) the differences in culture, I relish the nuances, the strange anomalies of language. We laugh together over the comical misunderstandings. When I'm asked if I want "hot tea", I'm tempted to reply, "Of course! Tea *is* hot!" But no, they have a horrible travesty of our sacred drink: iced tea! Greatly to be deplored!

There is so much I love and admire about America. But although I have spent a lot of time here, I don't belong. I may be in it, but I am not of it. I belong across the Pond, in another country; and when I see on the television my fellow Brits cheering their Queen, and when I see her on that balcony – small, silver-haired, undeniably old but still indefinably regal – my heart swells with pride and I have a lump in my throat and a longing to be there too.

As the old negro spiritual expressed it, "This world is not my home, I'm just a passin' through." We belong somewhere else, in another kingdom ruled by another King. I am in the world, but not of it. There is this strange dichotomy. The more I see of the world, the more I marvel at its diversity and its beauty. This is the world God has created for his glory and delight! It's right to love it. And yet, and yet… deep down there is a longing for Another Country. We have been born again into a different kingdom and our hearts want it.

Sometimes we see it manifested clearly: acts of kindness, acts of compassion; people humbly loving each other, learning to live together, sharing their lives because they have this in common: they love and serve the King. Sometimes it is tangible, as in a worship service when voices are raised as one in adoration, and you feel a surge of emotion; and if you try to analyse it, you can only think, "He is wonderful! And this is where I feel at home!"

It's in the community of the redeemed that the rule and reign of the King is manifested; and it is out from there that the message of his kingship goes forth. There are many references scattered throughout the Bible to a King ruling in righteousness, whose sceptre, the symbol of justice, will hold sway among the nations. From Genesis onwards, prophecy unfolds about this One: "The sceptre will not depart from Judah... until he to whom it belongs shall come, and the obedience of the nations shall be his" (Genesis 49:10); "Your throne, O God, will last for ever and ever; a sceptre of justice will be the sceptre of your kingdom" (Psalm 45:6).

When Queen Elizabeth was crowned in Westminster Abbey on 2 June 1953, she was handed a bejewelled orb surmounted by a cross. Holding a golden sceptre in the other hand, denoting the rule of justice, she was anointed with oil, and made vows to rule with justice and righteousness, according to God's holy laws. In reality, her influence has declined drastically. But it is still impressive to see old film footage of that ceremony. Human monarchy should be a reflection (however dim) of the supreme sovereignty of the King of Kings.

The theologian Eldon Ladd wrote a book about the kingdom of God and explained it this way: "The kingdom is now, and not yet." The kingdom of God is among us, but has not fully come. We live in an overlapping period when sometimes Jesus' rule breaks out, but often is unseen or unknown. When we see it we love it!

Keep praying, "Let your kingdom come, Lord!" until we see the final glorious manifestation of it. Until then, like Abraham, we see the City, dimly, from a distance (Hebrews 11:10).

Treasures of Darkness

Terry and I were driving in the mountains of Colorado. As we drove higher, we kept seeing mounds of gravel and debris, old pitheads and gaping mine entrances, and rusty, abandoned machinery. Eventually we reached Leadville, an historic mining city, and also the highest city in USA. The sign as we entered proclaimed the elevation to be 10,430 feet. In the days of its former glory, it was a city of over 30,000 people, a centre of life and culture, and even boasted an opera house.

Now it has shrunk to a main street lined with ancient shops filled with fascinating bric-a-brac from days gone by (guns and ammunition, sheriffs' badges, saddles and spurs), a wonderful old saloon complete with a long wooden bar and swing doors, and a few art galleries. We chatted with an ancient and picturesque character who claimed to have ridden bulls in rodeos as well as working down the mines.

We drove on through the breathtaking terrain to another, more modern, town called Breckonridge, and eventually over the Loveland Pass, which claims to be the highest drivable road in the USA, and is only open in summer when there is no snow. All through these mountains we saw evidence of old mine-workings. Gold, silver, copper, lead and coal were all mined years ago. Some mining still continues, but on a much smaller scale.

It was, of course, the discovery of gold which caused the famous Gold Rush of the early years of the last century. Massive fortunes were made, and often quickly lost in gambling and bad investments. But in the early 1930s gold declined drastically in value, and overnight, millionaires became paupers.

We heard of a father who would descend the mine each day before daylight and emerge each evening after the sun had set, thus spending most of his life in the dark. His sons followed him. What an unnatural life! What compels men to do that? Simply, the lure of riches. As soon as the news got out about the discovery of another seam of gold, prospectors would pour in like lemmings to stake a claim.

In a prophecy of Isaiah to a king called Cyrus, God said, "I will give you the treasure of darkness, riches stored in secret places" (Isaiah 45:3). In the context, this could mean literally gold, silver, and gems mined out of the earth. But God has other treasures which he promises to share with his children. What are these treasures?

Blessed are those who find wisdom…
she is more profitable than silver and
yields better returns than gold. She is
more precious than rubies; nothing you
desire can compare with her… Choose my
instruction instead of silver, knowledge
rather than choice gold… With me are
riches and honour, enduring wealth and
prosperity. My fruit is better than fine
gold; what I yield surpasses choice silver.

Proverbs 3:13–14; 8:10, 18–19

The early chapters of the book of Proverbs offer two alternatives: seeking wisdom or drifting into folly. But wisdom has to be intentionally sought after and looked for, like treasure. These chapters use words such as "Seek", "Turn your ear", "Apply your heart", "Call out for", "Search for". Effort and energy are involved, but the rewards are great, for when wisdom is found, it provides protection, a shield of security for life's journey. Material riches are ephemeral, fleeting, uncertain; wisdom comes from God and is his precious gift.

Better to dig for wisdom than gold! Wisdom is an investment which will bring eternal rewards.

Being Heard

I was reading about Hannah in the Old Testament. She was in a very dysfunctional family; she was infertile, introspective, and depressed; she felt isolated and unfulfilled. One day she ran into the temple and poured out her misery to God. The priest, Eli, misunderstood and thought she was drunk. Obviously he was not used to people praying in such an uninhibited way!

Tearfully, she protested that she was praying out of grief. Eli then gave her a very simple, direct word: "Go in peace, and may the God of Israel grant you what you have asked of him" (1 Samuel 1:17). Basically, "Don't worry, you have been heard."

The effect was dramatic. She straightened up, her depression lifted and her face changed. No longer creased and blotched with tears, it reflected the peace that now flooded her. Her appetite returned, and her heart, formerly obsessed with her inner fears and feelings, now turned towards her husband. Their marriage was renewed and she conceived! That was quite a lot of healing, in fact! She was set free by a word of reassurance that she had been heard.

People pay a lot of money to be heard. They go and lie on a couch and talk to a shrink: they pour out their memories, their anger, their frustration, and it is questionable as to whether much is achieved. But they are desperate to have someone listen to them.

David the Psalmist cried out to God frequently. He knew God was a trustworthy recipient of his deepest fears and feelings: "Trust in him at all times, you people; and pour out your hearts to him" (Psalm 62:8). David knew he was heard. "In my distress I called to the Lord; I cried to my God for help. From his temple he heard my voice; my cry came before him, into his ears" (Psalm 18:6).

Imagine a majestic throne. Myriads of angels are worshipping; the noise is thunderous. The One on the throne is wearing a headset. Suddenly he makes a gesture: "Quiet, everyone!" A weak signal is coming right into his ears: "Help!" Immediately he responds. Machinery is set in motion, big artillery is wheeled out, battle-lines are drawn, hostilities commence. Things are happening in heavenly places that David has no comprehension of (Psalm 18:6–15).

We don't know the power that our prayers can unleash. In fact, often we are not even sure that we have been heard! Lots of Christians think God hasn't heard them, or he is deaf, or indifferent. But he does hear. His ear is always tuned into his children. Because you didn't get an immediate answer, or didn't get the answer you wanted, doesn't mean that you were not heard.

There is only one context in which God does not listen. "If I had cherished sin in my heart, the Lord would not have listened" (Psalm 66:18). "Cherish" is a strong word: it means we love, nurture, cultivate, and protect something. If you are "cherishing" sin, you are deliberately and tenaciously indulging in an activity which is contrary to God's way. Not good: you won't be heard by God while you are doing that. But "a broken and contrite heart you, God, will not despise" (Psalm 51:17). If you have sinned but are truly repentant, he forgives, and hears, and relationship is restored. David knew this, even after committing the grossest sins.

In reality, most Christians are seeking to walk with God, to obey him, and to please him; they are not living in deliberate disobedience. But many Christians beat themselves, thinking they must have sinned, because God apparently is not listening to them. False logic! The Father listens to the child. In Christ, you are a child of God.

He may take time over the answer. In Psalm 18, it seems there was a big fight in the heavenlies before the enemy was routed, and then, "He reached down from on high and took hold of me... He brought me into a spacious place; he rescued me because he delighted in me" (verses 16, 19). It may be that while we are pouring out our hearts to God, he is removing things that are hampering his will, getting the conditions right, waiting for the perfect timing. But the answer will never be too late. And it may not be quite what you expected.

But know this: he hears the weakest, most despairing cry; he hears strong petitions and tears; he hears pain and confusion. In fact, he is the best person on whom to pour it all out, because he won't repeat it, he won't judge you, and he won't turn away. He is, unlike Eli, a sympathetic High Priest. You have been heard.

"Let us then approach God's throne of grace with confidence, so that we may receive mercy and find grace to help us in our time of need" (Hebrews 4:16).

Called

I wanted to be "called".

I was raised in a Christian family, familiar with the concept of lives devoted to Christ. Many of my relatives were missionaries or church leaders of some sort.

One of the things they all had in common, it seemed, was that they had a "call": some momentous day when they knew God had picked them out to be involved in some kind of service for him. Then they would proceed to the "mission field" (which in my childish imagination I saw as a big green meadow with canvas tents pitched in it, from which missionaries would sally forth with large bundles of tracts to evangelize the heathen!).

I wanted to serve God; therefore it appeared I had to have a call. In my thinking, this was akin to receiving a gilt-edged invitation card with the name of a place or country (the further away the better) written on it in Gothic lettering. In fact, the further away and more exotic it was, the more authentic the call… or CALL!

I went to Bible college and waited. Surely God

would be glad to give me a call.

Once or twice I tried to manoeuvre a call, but frustratingly, God didn't seem impressed, didn't want me in those places, and by my third year, I was perplexed. To add to my confusion, a young man kept hovering around in a disturbing fashion. I asked him a couple of times, politely, to move out of the way, because I was trying to find God's will for my life. The thing was, when I pictured myself in some heroic situation on the "mission field", I also imagined that I would write to him, keep in touch… I didn't want to lose him entirely. As a friend, of course.

Then one day as I was studying for my finals, and gazing out of the window, God suddenly spoke to me. It wasn't in Gothic letters, but it was soft and clear and went straight to my heart: "Terry Virgo is my will for your life."

It's interesting how God causes us to love his will! I was very happy about this! I have been serving God in the capacity of Terry's wife for over forty years now. It has been a happy, exciting and fruitful "call".

What is a "call"? Is it a biblical concept? Does everyone need one? Jesus called his disciples; Paul knew he was called to be an apostle. What about the rest of us? Some things we are *all* called to. God has called us into fellowship with his Son, Jesus Christ (1 Corinthians 1:9). We are called to one hope (Ephesians 4:4). God calls us into his kingdom and glory (1 Thessalonians 2:12). We are called to a holy life (1 Peter 1:15), called into a New Covenant (Hebrews 9:15), called out of darkness into his glorious light (1 Peter 2:9).

It seems to me that we are all called to participate in the glorious benefits that Jesus has made available to us through the cross and resurrection. As we believe the gospel, in Christ all these blessings accrue to us. But it is manifestly true that as we walk on with Jesus, he leads us into particular contexts and activities with the goal of bearing fruit for him.

So how do we find our calling? I think we make this unnecessarily complicated. It is as if we view his calling as a kind of tightrope that needs particular skill and balance to walk on successfully, or we will fall off and be disqualified. And that's if we can find it in the first place! However, mostly, if we just carry on doing what we are doing, seeking to please him and be fruitful where we are, he has promised to be with us, and will make it plain if he has new instructions; that is, he will call us out into something fresh.

Knowing that we are "called", into whatever branch of service, has several advantages:

- Firstly, it reinforces our belief that we are not our own: we are not here to please ourselves, but to serve a Master.

- Secondly, it defines our mission: you are to go *there*, to do *that*.

- Thirdly, it gives purpose and meaning to our life and labour.

- Fourthly, it authorizes us to act and make decisions.

- Fifthly, it means we have grace to do the job.

- Lastly, when we are opposed, fed up, and discouraged, we can take heart from the fact that this was not our bright idea; we are acting on behalf of the King, and he is responsible for what happens to us.

Jesus himself knew what it was to be called:

- He often referred to being sent by the Father.

- He knew he had come to seek and save the lost and reconcile them to God.

- He was not meandering through life randomly: he had come to accomplish the Father's will.

- He acted with authority, because he and the Father were in agreement.

- When he was tempted to turn aside, he set his face like flint to go to his destiny.

Basically, we are all called to serve God and bear fruit for him. This may be as a teacher, a mother, a librarian, a nurse, a preacher… whatever. Some people are called to spectacular walks in life, and we look at them and sigh wistfully, and wonder if we missed it somewhere.

Don't wish for someone else's calling. Pursue your own with faith, relying on God's energizing and sufficient grace.

Trained for War

I had a free day and needed to spend time with the Lord. I went to the attic room at the top of the house with my Bible and a notebook, and asked the Holy Spirit to guide me. After a while I found myself transfixed by Psalm 18. I saw how David was in a tight spot, vulnerable and afraid. He cried out to God in his desperation, and his weak cry came right into God's ears. God responded dramatically: he rescued David, and then began a process of training. By the end of the psalm, David was transformed into a brave and seasoned warrior.

Verse 34 says, "He trains my hands for battle". That day I asked God if I could enrol in his training programme. There did not seem to be an immediate answer, but looking back, I can see how he began to prepare me for some warfare that lay ahead.

There came a time when I had a big issue to pray about. A situation had gone on for several years. Of course, we had prayed, but now I sensed it was time for some direct confrontation. Now warfare was a reality, not a Bible study. I was able to set aside a few days for specific prayer and fasting.

On the Sunday afternoon, I was encouraged by Joshua 3:5: "Consecrate yourselves, for tomorrow the Lord will do amazing things among you." Time to get ready! The Holy Spirit nudged me to inspect my weapons. I collected several promises, Bible references, and prophetic words that we had received over years. I felt as if I were laying them out in a line in the grass and walking around them; then picking them up, polishing them and reminding myself of their significance. These were to be my arrows. Psalm 45:5 said: "Let your sharp arrows pierce the hearts of the king's enemies". This wasn't primarily my battle, then: it was God's. My enemies were his enemies. This reinforced my faith and was exhilarating, because I knew we were going into battle together!

The next day, I began with worship, reminding myself of our all-powerful and loving King. Over the next few days, I knelt, I lay on the floor, I walked up and down, declaring God's word, speaking truth, often directly to the enemy. He must release this person who belonged to Jesus, because he had no right to devour and destroy the King's property. The word of God was my sword to thrust and lunge with. The promises were my arrows to shoot into the ranks of the enemy. As I did this, I was often aware that another, stronger hand was over mine, pulling back the bowstring, guiding the arrow to find the target. Sometimes I sang warring songs, sometimes I spoke in tongues when I had no more words in English.

I read that the word "revelation" is *apokalepsis* in Greek (from this we get the English word "apocalypse"). Made up of two words, *apo* and *kalepsis*, it literally means "to take away a veil". That is what revelation is: the removing of a veil or covering to reveal something hidden. We are told that the enemy has blinded people to truth by flinging a veil over their minds (2 Corinthians 4:4). So I prayed for Jesus to take off the veil that had brought confusion and blindness in this situation.

It was an intense five days: and then suddenly, breakthrough! God reached down his hand and personally rescued the one who had been in such peril. He spoke into his heart, pulled the veil off his mind, and with infinite love, rescued and restored him.

There is no formula for prayer warfare, but there are some tried and tested truths:

- Remember, the battle is the Lord's – so it must be fought as he directs.

- His word is powerful, and we can declare it with authority.

- He is faithful to his promises.

- We do not know how long or short the battle may be; and there may be different seasons and phases in it.

• It is always God's will to set captives free.

I also learned that it is really God who does all the work; but he graciously allows us to get into the fight with him, and share in the spoils of victory!

Under the Umbrella

We left Atlanta, Georgia, in crushing heat. The temperature was 106 degrees Fahrenheit; it hurt to breathe, and it was impossible to be outside for more than a few minutes. We had been in America for over five weeks, and most of the time, wherever we were – Missouri, Oklahoma, Colorado, Illinois – the temperatures were unusually and persistently high. As I write, fires are ravaging the forests of Colorado.

For poor old Britain, languishing in the wettest, coldest June (in summer 2012) since records began, such temperatures are the stuff of dreams. Oh, to feel the warmth of the sun, to be able to go out without being armed with macs and umbrellas, to be able to have picnics and barbecues and not be blue and shivering; not to mention sporting events where rain doesn't stop play, and weddings where the bride's mother can be sure that her hat isn't ruined, and the guests can wear floaty summer frocks instead of sweaters and coats!

As we flew in over London, the pilot intoned the ritual greeting: "Good morning, welcome to London, where the temperature is 15 degrees Centigrade and it is raining…" The temperature varies slightly from time to time, but it is usually raining when we arrive at any time of the year. No, I am not moaning, just stating the facts.

Our friends in hot countries are always amused by the Brits' relentless desire to go out in the sun, not appreciating that we hardly ever see it. I remember being in Germany once with an international group of people, and it began to snow. The Africans and Indians among us were ecstatic! They rushed out and rolled around in it, laughing idiotically. Well, that's how we feel about the sun.

Terry and I decided to walk along by the river at Kingston and eat at a pub. It was only drizzling a bit, but by the time we went out, the rain was more persistent, and the tennis at Wimbledon was postponed yet again. We unfurled the enormous golfing umbrella we keep in the car and walked along the riverbank. Actually, it was fun. It was good to be together, walking hand in hand back in good old England. Lots of swans were swimming about and several boat crews were out on the water, where raindrops were spattering the surface.

Later we went to the church prayer meeting. We were aware once again of being under the umbrella of God's presence and love for his people. But it was also good to reflect that we have been under it in our travels, sheltered by his loving hand in desert places, on mountain-tops, in cities, in airports.

Here the grass is green, the trees are leafy and the gardens are full of colour. Flowers that I had planted before I left are blooming in their pot in the front garden. The bad news is that the weeds are merrily flourishing too! England is a green, if not always pleasant, land.

Cool Britannia!

Two Sheepdogs

Are you one of those people who are always looking back over their shoulder, afraid of something creeping up behind them? Financial disaster will overtake you; your mother had Alzheimer's, so you are bound to end up like her; your cousin died of cancer, it's in the family, it's only a matter of time before you discover the ominous lump; your father had a heart attack at the age of sixty – only a year to go until you are the same age...

Some people live in fear and negativity, always expecting the worst.

There is good news. When you are born again into God's family, you inherit a different outlook on the future. Your earthly family may have lived under the shadow of death, but you have been brought into everlasting life. You now have a Good Shepherd who leads you beside still waters, in green pastures. Not only that, he has two sheepdogs called Goodness and Mercy who run behind the flock, keeping the sheep from evil predators, nudging them into the right path.

Even when the enemy presses uncomfortably close, we need not be afraid, because the Shepherd is walking purposefully ahead. He is not planning on being ambushed. In fact, he has planned a picnic, a table spread in full view of the enemy! He really expects us to sit down and enjoy eating and drinking in a leisurely fashion with him, and not worry about the threat of the guns blazing over the hill!

This doesn't mean that we are in denial about opposition: "Let's just shut our eyes, and perhaps it will go away." No; the opposition forces are real enough; they are very strong, but not omnipotent. David was quite candid about this: "My foes… were too strong for me. They confronted me in the day of my disaster, but the Lord was my support. He brought me out into a spacious place; he rescued me because he delighted in me" (Psalm 18:17–19).

As Christians, we are not exempt from the sort of disasters which assail everyone; but we do not have to live our lives in fear and dread of what might happen. We live our lives in the knowledge that we are encapsulated by God's love. "You hem me in behind and before, and you lay your hand upon me" (Psalm 139:5).

Those two sheepdogs are chivvying us along, running ahead, nudging us from behind, keeping us on track. Even if we fall over or get injured, the Shepherd whistles to them: "Hey! Goodness! Mercy! Go get!" They run up behind, snuffling at our heels, reassuring us that we are not forgotten, and the Shepherd is nearby. He will never leave us or abandon us, and walks with us through the darkest valley.

"This I know, God is *for* me" (Psalm 56:9).

The Shadow of Your Wings

David wrote, "I long to dwell in your tent for ever and take refuge in the shelter of your wings" (Psalm 61:4). But camping is not my preferred way of life. I know that modern tents come with all sorts of luxuries and ingenious gadgets which, I am sure, are meant to deceive us into thinking that we are actually quite happy, comfortable, and at home in one. No, no! However your surroundings are contrived, there is still nothing between you and the elements but a thin sheet of canvas or polyester!

A tent is not a safe, permanent, solid structure. It is cold at night, it gets damp inside at the slightest drizzle, everything has to be stored on the ground, cooked on the ground, eaten on the ground... unless you bring in truckloads of furniture, which to me, defeats the whole point. If you want furniture, stay in a Holiday Inn. Camping is supposed to be simple and basic.

Tents, let's face it, are meant to be temporary. They speak of here today, gone tomorrow; a nomadic existence; in short, mobility.

It's interesting, then, that David says in this

psalm that he longs to dwell in God's tent. In the wilderness years, the Ark of God, which was the symbol of his presence among his people, was kept in the Tabernacle, which was a tent-like structure designed to be taken down quickly when the cloud moved on and Israel had to decamp. So here, David is saying that he wants to be constantly living in God's presence. But God didn't stay in one place, and when he moved on, so did the Israelites.

However, David also says he wants to "take refuge in the shelter of your wings". "Wings" doesn't conjure up a sense of safety. It seems a strange metaphor to use. If anything, it evokes a sense of danger, not refuge. Freewheeling in the atmosphere is what birds do; it is not a natural environment for us humans. On the whole, we tend to think of a "refuge" as a solid, immovable place like a fortress – heavily defended, impregnable. But in this psalm, God's protection is seen as being deployed while on the move. He intends his people to have mobility in their hearts; they are not supposed to get static, stuck, immobilized.

In Romans 4:16, Paul says that all those who live by faith are children of Abraham. Abraham was definitely one whose lifestyle was mobility. God called him, and he "obeyed and went, even though he did not know where he was going... he lived in tents" (Hebrews 11:8–9). He was the first of many whom God called to be on a journey with him. This is in the

DNA of Christians; not necessarily for geographical journeying, although it often is; but to have readiness in their hearts that they could be called at any time to anywhere, to new horizons, new ventures of faith.

(Of course, you could live in the same place for years, but be facing massive challenges which require courageous re-evaluation and fresh decisions.)

Therefore we must not put our roots down too deeply or too firmly, or it will be a traumatic operation to pull them up, if the call should come.

There is greater mobility across the globe today than at any other time in history. Often people move for economic reasons, or because of political unrest, or cruel regimes, or desires to join family, or to find a more congenial environment. The reasons are numerous. But for the children of God, whatever the presenting circumstance, it must be because the King has willed it. This is what drove many valiant men and women to relocate around the world, risking lives and health, reputation and wealth. When I read the biographies of these intrepid heroes, I am amazed at their reckless courage and devotion to Jesus. They measured safety in a different way.

The strange thing is that moving because *God* says so is the safest thing to do, because it is under his protection. His wings are spread over us. The cloud has moved on: better to move with it than be left behind, with no tent, no wings stretched above us!

It takes courage; it takes faith. I am constantly in awe of the brave decisions that many of my Christian friends have made to move from somewhere comfortable and familiar to an environment that has a different climate, culture, and demographic; which involves dealing with economic challenges, family upheaval, and painful goodbyes to friends and relatives. But they know that those wings are flapping around them, and the presence of God goes with them as they move their "tents" for the next stage of the journey.

Which is better – to be mobile but covered, or static but unsheltered?

Pillars in the House of God

*D*avid wrote, "Our daughters will be like pillars carved to adorn a palace" (Psalm 144:12). We know that he had lots of sons, but we don't read much about his daughters. We know he had some; but why would he want them to be like pillars? An upright column, stuck to the floor? It seems a strange ambition to have for them. But it could be a good metaphor for a Christian woman.

A pillar must be strong; there is no point to a pillar which is weak and crumbling! Does God want strong women? I am sure he does; but not strong in the sense of being pushy and aggressive. "Be strong *in the Lord*," counsels Paul in Ephesians 6:10. So we are not talking about strength of personality or physical strength or assertiveness. He taught the churches to be strong in faith, in love, and in the grace that is in Christ Jesus.

This last is especially important. To be strong in grace means that we are convinced of the truth that we can do nothing to earn our salvation. Jesus has done all that is necessary to save us from the power and the penalty of sin; we need to be able to stand on that truth and withstand the attacks of the devil, who loves to accuse us, to bring us under guilt and condemnation.

We also need to be strong to withstand the lies and distortions that are prevalent today in relation to Godly femininity. Marriage and motherhood are God-given roles to be prized, nurtured, and protected. There is an "inner beauty" that pleases God and brings honour to him, as well as being comfortable with our physical femininity and appearance (1 Peter 3:1–6).

Pillars also have to be straight! If they are leaning over, they will cause the building to be shaky. As Christian women we must be straightforward and honest, not devious. We are to be "blameless and pure, 'children of God without fault in a warped and crooked generation'" (Philippians 2:15). Jesus comes to make the crooked straight.

Stability is another obvious attribute. If a pillar is wobbly, it threatens the stability of the whole structure. "Stand firm in the faith" (1 Corinthians 16:13). We need to be uncompromising, focused, not double-minded.

What else? The function of pillars is to be supportive. They are integral to the structure, whether visible or hidden. They hold up the ceiling! We need to have respect for those who have leadership responsibility, for husbands in the home, for elders in the church. Do the leaders in our churches and families know that we are there for them, encouraging them, cheering them on? Do they feel our love and respect? It is so easy to cause energy to leak away from the centre by being negative, complaining, and undermining.

We also need to develop our own gifting so that the body of Christ can be enriched and rounded out. Gifts of wisdom, teaching, hospitality, prophecy, and serving can all be used to strengthen the whole.

So pillars all have to be strong, straight, stable, and supportive, but they don't all have to look the same! In Solomon's house there was a room panelled with cedar, and it had forty-five cedar wood pillars (1 Kings 7). Imagine the fragrance of that room! Then there were two bronze pillars at the entrance of the temple. They must have been dazzling when the sun hit them! Some pillars were also very decorative, carved with lilies and pomegranates.

There is something awesome about rows of pillars in a magnificent cathedral. In St Peter's in Rome, the pillars are massive, soaring up into the high, vaulted ceiling. Standing there in their immovable rows, the light falling on them and creating complex shadows, they are solemn, grand, majestic, bringing beauty and strength to the great historic structure.

So can we; for we are not part of just any old building. As we stand together, united in purpose, strong in the Lord, straight and true, we can bring honour to the King and adorn his house.

Float Trip

*I*t was a glorious day! The sunshine filtered through the green canopy overhead and the water rippling over the smooth stones was clear and inviting. I took a paddle, clambered into the canoe, and took the front seat. Terry pushed off from the shore, climbed in and sat in the back. The boat glided forward. We were off! Once again, as I have over many years, I experienced a little bubble of joy and excitement as we set off on another float trip.

Sometimes people ask us what activities we enjoy, and we casually mention that we like canoeing. It sounds very adventurous and daring and athletic. What we actually mean is that we love a leisurely day floating down a beautiful river in Missouri with our friends. It doesn't require too much effort: some judicious paddling over the fast bits, which we laughingly call "the rapids"; some careful negotiating of submerged logs and rocks here and there; and the rest of the time serenely floating along, being carried on the current.

It is quite an expedition to mount, and our good friend Alleta usually takes care of all the organization: phoning ahead to book the boats, checking on the weather, making sure we have plenty of drinks, and that everyone has suitable shoes for wading in the water. She also packs massive cooler chests with enough sandwiches and fruit to sustain an expedition to the Gulf of Mexico. On the few occasions when we have had to cancel because of storms or because the river has been dangerously high, it has been a sharp disappointment!

We gather for breakfast first and then load up the cars. About an hour later than planned, we drive off to the river. We usually have to stop somewhere to buy something or wait while someone goes back for something they have forgotten. Eventually we arrive at the river. We park the cars and unpack our provisions (including lots of sun lotion, battered old hats for some, and baseball caps for others), and then pile into a rickety bus that takes us to a point some miles upstream. From there, we put into the water, and float back to where we started, sore and sunburned.

So, why is it so good? For a start, the Niangua river in Missouri is beautiful. We floated down a river in Arkansas once, and it was also glorious. Of course, conditions vary. If it has rained a lot, the river is high and it can be more exciting and hazardous. Terry and I tipped over once, trying to negotiate a sharp bend; usually someone flips their boat, but it's part of the fun. If there has been little rain, it can be too shallow and the boat has to be dragged over some gravelly places. Last June, it was perfect! The water was clear, the current strong but not difficult, and because the weather had been settled, there was not much debris.

One of the features is watching the wildlife. Often a blue heron flies just ahead of us, flapping its wide, blue-grey wings. We see fish darting about in the water, and any kids with us usually find a few crawdads: little prawn-like creatures similar to the crayfish native to England. Sometimes we have seen water snakes, and turtles line up on tree branches near the surface and plop in as we pass.

There are lovely wide stretches where the water moves slowly; there are deep pools where we jump in and swim; and there are narrow places and bends where the current quickens and we have to watch out for rocks and overhanging branches. Sometimes the river flows beneath high rock bluffs and we see hawks circling above.

We select an attractive "beach" and stop for lunch. Everyone gets out and we spread the feast. Then we swim, chat, play in the water, fish for crawdads, and eventually resume our leisurely journey, the sun now hot on our backs. Everyone has stories of past trips, mostly of boats overturning, or of being caught in torrential rain, or of getting stuck somewhere. These, of course, become more extravagantly remembered with the passing years.

I suppose we enjoy it so much because it's so

different from anything we do in England. It's unique to our enjoyment of being in America. The combination of sun, a beautiful river, trees, good friends, physical activity that is not too demanding but enough to make you feel pleasantly tired – all of these combine to create a happy and fulfilling day. The sort of thing to dream about on a cold, wet night in January!

I could make a good case for this being a metaphor for life; the parallels are obvious but rather cliché ridden, so I will just content myself with saying: "Thank you, Lord, for so many happy memories, not only of float trips, but all through my life's journey."

I am blessed.